Lucy E. Textor

Official Relations Between the United States and the Sioux Indians

Lucy E. Textor

Official Relations Between the United States and the Sioux Indians

ISBN/EAN: 9783337061845

Printed in Europe, USA, Canada, Australia, Japan

Cover: Foto ©Suzi / pixelio.de

More available books at **www.hansebooks.com**

LELAND STANFORD JUNIOR UNIVERSITY PUBLICATIONS

HISTORY AND ECONOMICS

2

OFFICIAL RELATIONS

BETWEEN THE

UNITED STATES AND THE SIOUX INDIANS

BY

LUCY E. TEXTOR, M. A.

PALO ALTO, CALIFORNIA
PUBLISHED BY THE UNIVERSITY
1896

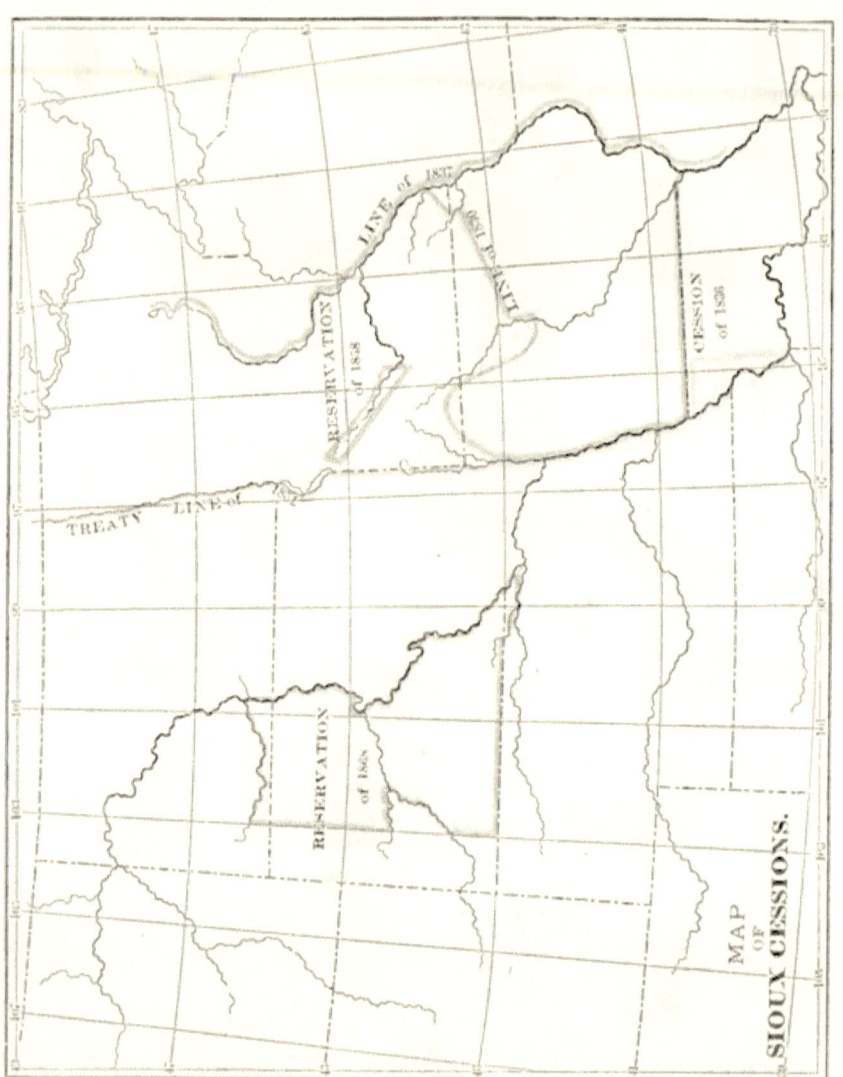

MAP 1.

MAP
OF
SIOUX CESSIONS.

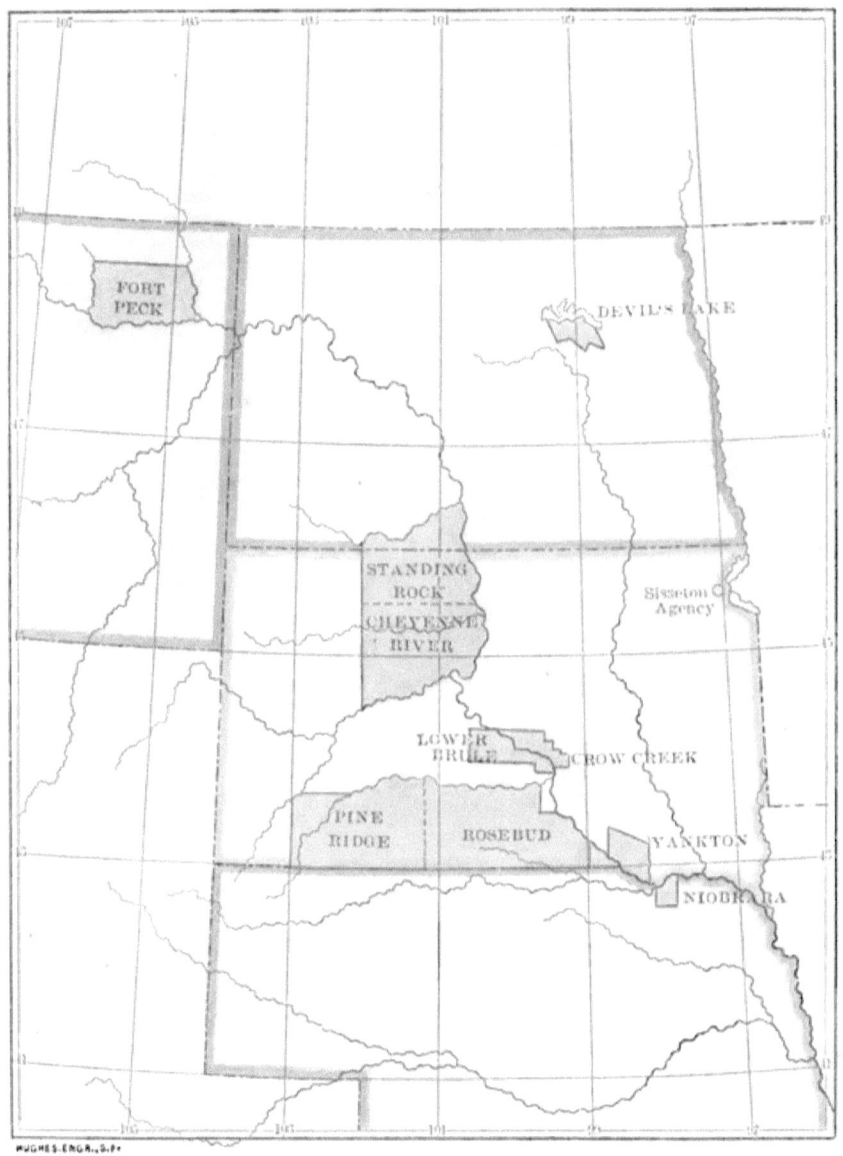

MAP SHOWING LOCATION OF THE SIOUX IN 1893.

MAP II.

LELAND STANFORD JUNIOR UNIVERSITY PUBLICATIONS

———

HISTORY AND ECONOMICS

2

———

OFFICIAL RELATIONS

BETWEEN THE

UNITED STATES AND THE SIOUX INDIANS

BY

LUCY E. TEXTOR, M. A.

PALO ALTO, CALIFORNIA
PUBLISHED BY THE UNIVERSITY
1896

EDITORIAL NOTE.

It is conceded that anything like an ideal general history of the United States is impossible until the whole field of investigation has been minutely explored by a host of separate workers. Indeed, it is in the production of a rapidly increasing monographic literature, comprising the results of such special research, that the American Universities are rendering a most useful service. The historical Seminary finds here its proper sphere. In the main, the materials for our social, institutional, and administrative history have yet to be gathered. Especially is this true of the relations of the Government with the red race. Before a complete and trustworthy account of its dealings with the Indian can be written, we must possess a detailed study of each tribe or group ; and who can doubt that the result of such a labor will be of the greatest sociological and ethical importance ? It is hoped that the publication of this tentative study of the Sioux will not be without value as a contribution to that result.

It remains to express the grateful acknowledgments of the Historical Department to Mr. Joseph Hutchinson, of Palo Alto, through whose generous appreciation Miss Textor's paper is now published.

G. E. H.

CONTENTS.

CHAPTER I.

An Outline of the Indian Policy of the United States.

CHAPTER II.

The Sioux from 1803 to 1850.

CHAPTER III.

The Sioux of the Mississippi from 1850 to 1893.

CHAPTER IV.

THE SIOUX OF THE PLAINS FROM 1850 TO 1893.

CHAPTER V.

THE YANKTONS.

CHAPTER VI.

STATUS OF THE SIOUX IN 1893.

Erratum.

Page 94, last line of text, for " Indians " read *Citizens.*

United States and the Sioux Indians.

CHAPTER I.

AN OUTLINE OF THE INDIAN POLICY OF THE UNITED STATES.

Probably no one would maintain that the United States, from the adoption of its Constitution to the present day, ever intentionally wronged the Indians ; but of the fact that it has wronged them there can be no question. This discrepancy is to a certain extent inherent in the very nature of the case. Not until we understood the character of the Indians and of our own civilization could we adopt a consistent attitude. But the mistake lay in the fact that no attempt was made to understand either, that we did not throw all the light of reason and scientific inquiry upon the problem and diligently apply ourselves to its solution. On the contrary, a policy of temporary expediency was adopted, to relieve evils which, unless otherwise treated, must remain permanent. It is true that we did not always regard this expediency as temporary, but we must have so regarded it, if we had not persistently closed our eyes to the facts of the case. Happily all this does not refer to the present policy. We are now earnestly studying the question, and, whatever the outcome, will have reason to believe that we have done our best.

Any discussion of our policy must be preceded by an inquiry into the recognized land rights of the Indians. This inquiry cannot be based upon the principles of abstract justice, for man's conception of these must vary with the age in which he lives, and the nineteenth century must find it a difficult matter to pass judgment upon the views of a less enlightened age. On the other hand, since the right of society to prescribe those rules by which property may be acquired and preserved cannot be drawn into question, and since the title of lands must be admitted to depend entirely on the nation in which they lie, it will be necessary to examine those principles which the Government has adopted in this particular case and which must be the basis of our decision.*

"On the discovery of this immense continent the great nations of Europe were eager to appropriate to themselves so much of it as they could respectively acquire. * * * But, as they were all in pursuit of nearly the same object, it was necessary, in order to avoid conflicting settlements and consequent war with each other, to establish a principle which all should acknowledge as the law by which the right of acquisition, which they all asserted, should be regulated as between themselves. This principle was, that discovery gave title to the government by whose subjects or by whose authority it was made against all other European governments, which title might be consummated by possession. The exclusion of all other

---

* Quoted in substance. Introduction to Indian Treaties : U. S. Statutes at Large, VII, 1.

Europeans necessarily gave to the nation making the discovery the sole right of acquiring the soil from the natives, and establishing settlements upon it. It was a right with which no European could interfere. It was a right which all asserted for themselves, and to the assertion of which by others all assented. * * * While the different nations of Europe respected the right of the natives as occupants, they asserted the ultimate dominion to be in themselves, and claimed and exercised as a consequence of this ultimate dominion a power to grant the soil while yet in possession of the natives. These grants have been understood by all to convey a title to the grantees, subject only to the Indian right of occupancy."*

The preceding extract from the opinion of Chief Justice Marshall in the case of Johnson *vs.* McIntosh is amply supported by history. France, Spain, Portugal, and Holland based their claim to American lands upon rights given by discovery, and no one of these powers gave its assent to this principle more unequivocally than did England.†

When the United States came into possession of the vast territories now included within its boundaries, it received also the rights by which these territories had previously been held.‡ It maintained, "as all others have maintained, that discovery gave an exclusive right to extinguish the Indian title of occupancy, either by

---

* Marshall, C. J., Johnson *vs.* McIntosh: Wheaton, VIII, 572 ff.

† See Introduction to Indian Treaties: U. S. Statutes at Large, VII, 2–6.

‡ *Ibid.*, 6–7.

purchase or by conquest; * and gave also a right to such a degree of sovereignty as the circumstances of the people would allow it to exercise."†

The original rights of the Indians were thus much impaired. Nevertheless, the tribes were looked upon as distinct, independent political communities. The term "nation" was applied to them, and the Constitution, by declaring the treaties already made and those to be made the supreme law of the land, admitted their rank among those powers capable of making treaties.‡ This inconsistency between fact and theory was recognized in the case, The Cherokee Nation *vs.* The State of Georgia. "It may well be doubted," we read here, "whether those tribes which reside within the acknowledged boundaries of the United States can, with strict accuracy, be denominated foreign nations. They may more correctly, perhaps, be denominated domestic dependent nations. They occupy a territory to which we assert a title, independent of their will, which must take effect in point of possession, when their right of possession ceases—meanwhile they are in a state of pupilage. Their relations to the United States resemble that of a ward to his guardian. They look to our Government for protection ; rely upon its kindness and its power ; appeal to it for relief to

---

* "Except only in the case of the Sioux Indians in Minnesota, after the outbreak of 1862, the Government has never extinguished an Indian title as by right of conquest; and in this case the Indians were provided with another reservation, and subsequently were paid the net proceeds arising from the sale of the land vacated": Report of the Commissioner of Indian Affairs for 1890, xxix.

† Introduction to Indian Treaties: U. S. Statutes at Large, VII, 7.

‡ See Worcester *vs.* The State of Georgia: Peters, VI, 519.

their wants ; and address the President as their Great Father."*

So much for the status of the Indians. We turn now to our early policy toward them. In order to understand the attitude of the Government during its first thirty years, it is necessary to have a clear conception of the condition of the thirteen original States. It is true that they possessed a broad territory of abundant resources, but it is equally true that their population occupied only a narrow belt along the Atlantic Ocean. Westward lay an unbroken wilderness. The valleys of the Tennessee and Ohio were one vast solitude, penetrated only by a few of the most hardy trappers. Even the frontier line extending from Maine to Georgia was undefended in many places and afforded the Indians copious opportunity to attack the white settlements. The States, therefore, must have keenly suffered in the face of a general Indian war.†

Yet such a war actually threatened them. The close of the Revolution found the Indians far from friendly to the new Republic. During the war with England there had been a continuous series of conflicts between the frontiersmen and their dusky neighbors. The latter had been continually "urged on by the British, who furnished them with arms, ammunition, and provisions, and sometimes also with leaders and with bands of auxiliary white troops, French, British, and tories."‡

---

* The Cherokee Nation *vs.* The State of Georgia : Peters, V, 1–2.

† For the condition of the States at this time, see McMaster, History of the People of the United States, I, 3–4.

‡ Roosevelt, Winning of the West, II, 373.

The peace of 1783 did not much improve the condition of affairs between these two hostile forms of society. The Indians continued their murders and depredations, and the whites their reprisals. The most fruitful sources of discord were indefinite boundary lines,* the trespass of the whites upon Indian lands in search of game,† and the attempt on the part of the States to increase their territory. On the other hand the Indians themselves were ready to rise at the least provocation and were spurred on to hostilities by England‡ and Spain.§

At this crisis fortune blessed the United States with a President better fitted than any one of his contemporaries to cope with this difficult state of affairs. In addition to an intimate and practical knowledge of the conditions of border life, George Washington was endowed with statesmanship of the highest order. He saw that the best interests of the two races demanded that they be kept apart, that inevitable conflict must result from the contact of the frontiersmen and the natives. Hence he discouraged the projection of isolated colonies into the western country, and urged that the barrier interposed between the white and the red men be made continuous, and the settlements to the east of that barrier compact.‖ The policy thus begun was followed by Wash-

---

* The act of May 19, 1796, provided that Indian boundary lines be definitely marked. See U. S. Statutes at Large, I, 469. Many of the treaties made with the various tribes between 1790 and 1820 contained a like provision. See U. S. Statutes at Large, VII, Index.

† Adams, History of the United States, VI, 70.

‡ American State Papers, Ind. Affrs., I, 480.

§ Ibid., 378; Lodge, George Washington, II, 92.

‖ Writings of Washington, X, 307.

ington's successors and found its best exponent in the
Intercourse Laws, which made the most rigid provision
for keeping the two races apart.*

Meanwhile, however, the present condition of affairs
had to be dealt with. War existed on the frontier, and
the Indians were loud in their accusations of ill treatment on the part of our Government and its people, and
fierce in their revenge of the wrongs committed against
them. Washington made use of every "reasonable
pacific measure"† to bring about peace ; and, for this
purpose, endeavored to check the spirit of speculation
in lands,‡ and to further the making of treaties which
should definitely settle boundary lines and place the
relations of the Government and the Indians upon a
firm basis. He was above all convinced that peace could
be secured and maintained only by treating the aborigines with strictest justice.§ But, should it be impossible
to end hostilities by conciliation, he was of the opinion
that "sound policy and good economy" pointed "to a
prompt and decisive effort, rather than to defensive and
lingering operations."‖

The principle of non-intervention was thus one of the

---

* See act of July 22, 1790 : U. S. Statutes at Large, I, 137-8 ; act of
March 1, 1793 : ibid., 329-32 ; act of May 19, 1796 : ibid., 469-74 ; act
of January 17, 1800 : ibid., II, 6-7 ; act of March 30, 1802 : ibid., 139-
46 ; act of April 29, 1816 : ibid., III, 332-3 ; act of March 3, 1817 : ibid.,
383 ; act of May 6, 1822 : ibid., 682-3.

† Writings of Washington, XI, 466.

‡ Ibid., XII, 70.

§ Ibid., XI, 466.

‖ Ibid. Despite the wisdom of Washington's policy it met with
much adverse criticism. See Abridgment of Debates, I, 341 ff ; Lodge,
Washington, II, 102-3.

main features of our early policy.   This principle recognized, as we have seen, the natural antagonism between
the two races and aimed to keep them apart.   But a certain amount of contact was inevitable and must increase
with the advance of our frontier.   It was Washington's
object to make these necessary relations as harmonious
as possible by attaching the Indians to our Government.
In his fifth annual address of December 3, 1793, he said :

   " Next to a vigorous execution of justice on the viola-
tors of peace, the establishment of commerce with the
Indian nations, on behalf of the United States, is most
likely to conciliate their attachment.   But it ought to be
conducted without fraud, without extortion, with constant
and plentiful supplies, with a ready market for the com-
modities of the Indians, and a stated price for what they
give in payment and receive in exchange.   Individuals
will not pursue such a traffic unless they be allured by
the hope of profit ; but it will be enough for the United
States to be reimbursed only."*

   These suggestions of Washington were afterwards embodied in the act of April 18, 1796,† authorizing the
establishment of trading-houses "for the purpose of
carrying on a liberal trade with the several Indian
nations," and appropriating $150,000 toward this end.
The act was originally passed for two years, but was
renewed‡ from time to time until 1822, when the Government trading-houses were abolished.§

---

* James, English Institutions and the American Indian, 36. In
connection with this subject, see also Writings of Washington, XII, 497.

† U. S. Statutes at Large, I, 452-3. Previous to this there had been
passed the act of March 3, 1795, appropriating $50,000 for the purchase
of goods to be sold to the Indians. See Annals of Congress, 1793-95, p. 1532.

‡ In 1802, 1803, 1806, and 1815.

§ U. S. Statutes at Large, III, 679-80.

The object of the factory system was two-fold : (1) to secure the friendship* of **the** Indians by supplying their wants ; (2) to supplant the British trader whose influence over the tribes was **at** that time very great.† These two ends were not attained. The Indians did not take kindly to Government trading, **and the English** trader was not dislodged.‡·

---

* In addition **to the** establishment of trading-houses there was other conciliatory legislation, as, for example, the act of May 13, 1800, authorizing the President to issue such rations as he should judge proper and as could be easily spared from the army provisions to Indians visiting the "military posts of the United States on the frontiers or **within** their respective nations." The President was furthermore empowered to defray the expenses of Indians visiting the seat of Government and to give them presents. U. S. Statutes at Large, II, 85.

† Annals of Congress, **4th** Cong., 1st Sess., 231. Later a third argument was advanced in favor of the factories. It was urged that they had a civilizing influence ; and Jefferson advocated that they be multiplied in order that those things might be placed within the reach of the Indians which would "contribute more to their domestic comfort than the possession of extensive, but uncultivated wilds." American State Papers, Ind. Affs., I, 684.

‡ The two chief reasons for this failure were these : **(1)** The Government licensed **private** traders who competed **with the** factories. (2) The advantages of the British trader were such **as** enabled him to maintain his supremacy. He had behind him the prestige of his government. English officers of the Indian Department were given military brevet rank, a fact of no mean importance considering **how** much Indians **are** influenced by a showy exterior, and English agents **were** required to **know at** least one Indian language. Furthermore, the British trader was allied **to his** customers by marriage, understood them well, sold them goods of a **superior** quality, **and gave credit.** The United States agents, on the other hand, were **often unfitted** for their positions and unreliable, were unable to adapt themselves to the Indians and sold them cheap goods at an enormous profit. American State Papers, Ind. Affs., II, 66, 79, 204 ; Wis. Hist. Colls., VII, 270–288; Abridgment of Debates, VII, 180 ff; Benton, Thirty Years' View, I, 20-1 ; Turner, Indian Trade in Wisconsin, 60 ; James, English Institutions and the American Indian, 39–42.

During these **years** the Government had not been entirely unmindful **of** civilizing the Indians. In its treaties with the **various** tribes it had used its influence to settle them **upon** restricted lands so that, no longer being able to subsist by the chase, they might be forced to farm, and it had **made provision to pay for the ceded** lands partly in agricultural implements.* As early as March 30, 1802,† Congress had passed **an** act authorizing **the Presi-**dent to expend not **more than $15,000** per annum " to promote civilization **among** the friendly Indian **tribes.''** Later the educational feature‡ was added, **and during the** years between 1818 and **1826 the number of children re-**ceiving instruction rose **from fifty to twelve hundred.§**

Such **were the main features of the early Indian** policy, non-intervention, friendship, and civilization. Of **the** fact that they were not always consistently carried out there can be **little** doubt. But the honest intentions of the United **States** can hardly be questioned. That the **Indians sometimes suffered injustice was due** largely to **the** inability **of the Central** Government always to control **the** conduct of individuals and States. The separate action of Georgia, as opposed to the Central Government, **gave** the first impulse to the removal policy.

The second stage of the national policy was inaugur-

---

* See treaties in U. S. Statutes at **Large, VII. A synopsis of those** made between 1789 and 1814 is given **in American State Papers, Ind.** **Affs.,** I, Index, lxxii–lxxvi.

† U. S. Statutes **at Large, II, 143.**

‡ **March** 3, 1819, **Congress** appropriated **$10,000** per annum for the payment of suitable persons to instruct the Indians in agriculture and to teach their children **reading,** writing, and arithmetic. U. S. Statutes at Large, III, 516–17.

§ American **State Papers, Ind. Affs., II, 700.**

ated by President Monroe in his message of January **27,**
1825.* Hitherto the course of the Government, as we
have seen, had been largely determined by expediency.
The United States now began to move upon a definite
system. Already in 1803, the year in which Louisiana
was purchased from France, the thought of colonizing
the Indians in this territory had occurred to the far-
seeing Jefferson. However, it had been vague in the ex-
treme and was associated with no well-defined system
to civilize the Indians, but was simply a desire to increase
their hunting privileges. It was reserved for President
Monroe definitely to inaugurate the removal policy. Its
main points according to the message of January 27,
1825,† were these : (1) Removal of the Indians from the
States and Territories east of the Mississippi ; (2) con-
veyance to them in fee simple of land west of the same
river ; (3) the establishment of an enlightened system of
internal government such as should gradually unite the
tribes ; (4) protection from the encroachments of our citizens. The immediate cause which influenced President
Monroe to deliver this message was Georgia's insistence
that the United States should fulfill its promise of 1802,
and extinguish the title to the Cherokee lands in her
State.‡ It was this same desire for more land on the part
of other States which brought about the removal policy.
This fact, however, was not put so boldly at the time.
The reasons given by those who favored a general removal of the tribes were two-fold. They said the pros-

---

* Statesman's Manual, I, 536–38.

† 18th Cong., 2nd Sess., No. 21.

‡ See Von Holst, Constitutional History of the United States, I,
433 ff.

perity of the United States and the welfare of the Indians depended upon it. All the various arguments which they brought forward to support their position were afterwards tersely put by President Jackson in his message of 1830. He said :

" The pecuniary advantages which it promises to the Government are the least of its recommendations. It puts an end to all possible danger of collision between the authorities of the general and State Governments, on account of the Indians. It will place a dense and civilized population in large tracts of country now occupied by a few savage hunters. By opening the whole territory between Tennessee on the north, and Louisiana on the south, to the settlements of the whites, it will incalculably strengthen the southwestern frontier, and render the adjacent States strong enough to repel future invasion without remote aid. It will relieve the whole State of Mississippi, and the western part of Alabama, of Indian occupancy, and enable those States to advance rapidly in population, wealth, and power. It will separate the Indians from immediate contact with the settlements of the whites ; free them from the power of the States ; enable them to pursue happiness in their own way, and under their own rude institutions ; will retard the progress of decay which is lessening their numbers ; and perhaps cause them gradually, under the protection of the Government, and through the influence of good counsels, to cast off their savage habits, and become an interesting, civilized, and Christian community."*

The message of President Monroe resulted in no im-

---

* Statesman's Manual, II, 745-6.

mediate legislation, though shortly afterwards the Creek
title to lands in Georgia was extinguished. The removal
policy was not formally adopted until May 28, 1830,
when Congress passed an act whose four main provisions
were as follows : The President was authorized (1) to
cause certain lands west of the Mississippi " to be divided
into a suitable number of districts, for the reception of
such tribes or nations of Indians as may choose to
exchange the lands where they now reside, and remove
there " ; (2) " to exchange any or all of such districts   *
*   *   with any tribe or nation of Indians now residing
within the limits of any of the States or Territories,   *
*   *   for the whole or any part   *   *   *   of the territory claimed or occupied by such tribe or nation " ; (3)
" solemnly to assure the tribe or nation with which the
exchange is made that the United States will forever
secure and guarantee to them, and their heirs or successors, the country so exchanged with them " ; (4) " to
cause such tribe or nation to be protected, at their new
residence, against all interruption or disturbance from
any other tribe or nation of Indians, or from any other
person or persons whatever."*

The foregoing act was supplemented by the Indian
Intercourse Act of June 30, 1834,† whose object was the
regulation of trade and intercourse with the Indian
tribes and the preservation of peace on the frontier.

* U. S. Statutes at Large, IV, 411–412. There were three other
sections authorizing the President to pay for improvements on ceded
lands ; to assist in the removal and render necessary aid in support for
the first year after the removal ; and to exercise the same superinten-
dence over the Indians as hitherto.   Still a fourth section appropriated
$500,000 to give effect to the act.

† *Ibid.*, 729–735.

The removal policy, as a policy, was then complete. It was not consummated as a fact, however, until 1842, by which time nearly all the tribes, with the exception of some unimportant fragments, had ceded their lands in the States and Territories east of the Mississippi and removed or agreed to remove west of that river.*

There was this difference between the scheme as planned by Jefferson and the policy as adopted by Congress. Jefferson made provision for a well-defined system of internal government and looked toward the civilization of the Indians as its ultimate goal ; Congress left the tribal government, as before, supreme, and took no definite steps toward the reclamation of the Indians from their wandering life. A wide area of land was given them and each individual was allowed to decide for himself whether he would be a nomad or a farmer, a decision which was likely to be influenced by the fact that the buffalo range was not far off.

The dates of the removal policy may be put down as 1825–38. There were removals before this time,† but they were determined by the exigencies of circumstances and made upon no fixed principle. There were removals after this time, but they were merely the carrying out of a principle whose spirit was dead, as those, for instance, between 1838 and 1850, or they were made necessary by the pressure of a white population upon the Indian country, as those of later years.

As a Government measure for the increase of State territory, the removal policy was a success : as a measure

---

* See the various treaties of session with the Indian tribes. U. S. Statutes at Large, VII, Index.

† See Hildreth, History of the United States, VI, 677–8.

for the promotion of the welfare of the Indians, it was a failure. The latter fact may be most easily seen in a study of the condition of the Creeks and Cherokees before and after their removal. They lost faith in civilization, and it was only after long years of hardship and suffering that they once more reached the plane which they had occupied in their former homes.

During the years between 1845 and 1855 events occurred which were to give the death-blow to the removal policy. In 1845 Texas* was admitted to the Union, and September 9, 1850, sold to the United States a portion of her territory now included in Kansas, Colorado, New Mexico, and the "public land strip."† In 1846 the long disputed Oregon question was settled, and the United States gained a perfect title to a large tract of land south of the forty-ninth parallel of north latitude and west of the Rocky Mountains.‡ In 1848, by the treaty of Guadaloupe Hidalgo, Mexico ceded to the United States lands now California, Nevada, Utah, and a part of Colorado, Arizona, and New Mexico.§ In 1853 the so-called Gadsden Purchase was made, and the United States came into possession of a strip of land containing forty-five thousand five hundred and thirty-five square miles, and now forming the southern part of the Territories of New Mexico and Arizona.‖

This immense increase of the public domain had a

* Donaldson, Public Domain, 12.

† *Ibid.*

‡ *Ibid.*, 7.

§ *Ibid.*, 12.

‖ *Ibid.*

direct bearing upon the Indian policy. Hitherto the
tribes had been kept upon our frontiers and pushed westward by the advancing tide of civilization. The
removal policy had contemplated the settlement of the
Indians upon lands where they should be free from contact with the whites. But the acquisition of new territory and the discovery of gold in 1848 so stimulated
immigration that the frontier line was broken. Whites
poured into the Indian country, and with such disastrous
consequences to the natives that it seemed necessary to take
immediate steps to save the border tribes from extinction.
It was thought that this could be done by a partial change
in the relative positions of the various tribes, which would
make it possible to throw open a wide extent of country
for the free spread of the white population westward.
It was for this purpose that the treaty of 1851 was made
with the Sioux of the Mississippi.

Again, with this increase of our territory came a proportionate increase in the magnitude of the Indian question. We had now a far greater number of tribes to deal
with than hitherto. Some mechanism of control was
imperatively necessary, and the reservation system was,
in part, devised to meet this need. The plan at first was
simply this : to locate the Indians as rapidly as possible
upon reservations whose extent should be proportionate
to their needs. If they could be induced to apply themselves to agriculture, the reservation might be small ; if
they must be allowed to hunt, it might be large. In
either case the Indians were to be brought into relationship with the United States through their agents.

Throughout the fifties emigration westward continued,

stimulated still further by the political troubles in Kansas. During these same years the national policy, perforce, assumed more definite form. With the wild Indians of the plains little, as yet, could be done, except to use every opportunity to settle them upon reservations. But the growing scarcity of game pointed to a solution. These tribes would soon be dependent upon the Government for food and could then be more easily held in check.

With those tribes who had by this time become somewhat used to an agricultural life, the policy was more definite. Two evils had marked our past treatment of them : the assignment of an unnecessarily large extent of land to be held in common, and the payment of large money annuities. An attempt was now made to remedy these evils. The three essential features of the plan were these : first, the location of the different tribes upon reservations only sufficiently large to satisfy their needs ; second, the allotment of this land in severalty to the Indians, requiring them to live upon and cultivate their individual allotments ; third, the payment of annuities in the form of stock, agricultural implements, mechanics' tools, and manual-labor schools.* This policy was first adopted with the Mississippi Sioux in 1858.†

The Indians of California were treated differently from all others. Neither Spain nor Mexico had ever acknowledged the usufructuary right of the aborigines to the land upon which they lived ; and it was held that when Mexico ceded this territory to the United States it had given

---

* This policy did not receive broad application during these years.

† See U. S. Statutes at Large, XII, 1037–41.

the Government an absolute title.*   The United States,
therefore, made no treaties with the Indians for the cession of lands, but settled them upon reservations established by executive order, which were to be run upon the
old mission plan.† The priests had gathered the Indians
upon tracts of land sufficiently large to yield them subsistence and had compelled them to cultivate the same.
The missions were thus self-supporting and often more
than that.   The place of the priest was now to be taken
by the agent, and the Indians were to be fed, clothed, and
civilized, without expense to the Government.   But the
plan refused to work, and the California reservations
were a miserable failure.‡

The decade between 1860 and 1870 was fruitful of discord.   There were Indian uprisings in all parts of the
country, and some of them were long and terrible. Never
before had the United States had so many men at one time
in the field against the hostiles, never had it fought more
bloody battles with them.   It would, of course, be difficult,
if not impossible, to trace out all the specific causes of these
wars.   That they were in part due to Indian "bad blood"

---

* Report of Commissioner of Indian Affairs for 1861-62 ; Sen. Docs.,
37th Cong., 2nd Sess., Vol. I, 637.

† As a matter of fact the Government had not sufficiently investi-
gated the mission plan.   It seems to have recognized only its excellen-
cies and to have been totally ignorant of its inherent evils.   Moreover it
did not take into consideration the fact that the priest labored for
himself, the agent for the Government, and that there might well be a
difference in the zeal displayed by the two.

‡ For a brief sketch of the California reservation system, see Report
of G. Bailey, Special Agent Interior Department, to Hon. Charles C. Mix,
Commissioner of Indian Affairs: Report of Commissioner of Indian
Affairs for 1858-9, pp. 649-657.

there can be no doubt ; but, on the other hand, this "bad blood" had been roused by the failure of the United States to keep its treaty obligations, and by the depredations of the whites, whose steady stream of immigration became visibly broader at the close of the civil war. Finally, June 20, 1867, Congress appointed a Commission* of seven members and authorized it to make treaties with the hostile tribes. The end in view was three-fold : first, the removal of the causes of war ; second, the security of our frontiers and the safe building of our western railroads ; third, the inauguration of some plan for the civilization of the Indians.

The Commission was also required to select a district or districts of country sufficiently large to accommodate all the Indian tribes east of the Rocky Mountains and not settled on reservations. These districts were to be made the permanent homes of such tribes.

The report of this Commission is interesting as a strong presentation of the Indian side of the question. It held that the causes of the wars of this decade lay wholly at the door of the Government, which had failed to keep its treaty stipulations and to protect the Indians from immigrants. The Indians had thus been obliged to take up arms in self-defense. The Commission made new treaties whose keeping, it said, would insure peace and the security of the frontiers and western railroads. The

---

* See U. S. Statutes at Large, XV, 17–18. This Commission was "to consist of three officers of the army not below the rank of Brigadier General, * * together with N. G. Taylor, Commissioner of Indian Affairs, John B. Henderson, Chairman of the Committee of Indian Affairs of the Senate, S. S. Tappan, and John B. Sanborn." The officers chosen from the army were Generals W. T. Sherman, W. S. Harney, and Alfred H. Terry.

terms of these treaties varied with the different tribes, but, as a whole, were in harmony with the governmental policy. They provided, in most cases, for the cession of Indian lands, the settlement of the Indians upon reservations, though with a privilege to hunt elsewhere, and the payment of annuities in goods.*

Finally, the Commission urged that all tribes east of the Rocky Mountains should be concentrated upon two large reservations, and should be provided with a territorial government. The wilder tribes should be allowed the privileges of the chase for the present, the others should cultivate the soil; and all should have annuities paid to them in the form of goods, only such a portion of these to be food as was absolutely necessary.†

The tone of this report was in strong contrast to the conduct of the War Department,‡ under whose control the Indians had in large measure fallen. The action of army officers was in certain specific cases deprecated; but the chief blame of our Indian troubles was laid at the door of our legislation, as being responsible for our wavering, inconsistent, and unjust Indian policy. The

---

* The treaty of 1868 with the Sioux is a good example. A synopsis of it is to be found in Chapter IV of this paper. For the treaties with the Kiowas and Comanches, Cheyennes and Arapahoes, and Shoshonees and Bannocks, see U. S. Statutes at Large, XV, pp. 581, 655, and 673, respectively.

† Report to the President by the Indian Peace Commission, January 7, 1868: Report of the Secretary of the Interior, 41st Cong., 2d Sess., 487 ff.

‡ Three members of the Commission were officers of the army, but a careful perusal of the report will serve to show that they had little to do with drawing it up. There is too great a gap between the sentiments of the report and the conduct of these gentlemen on the field of war.

recommendations of the Committee were such as seemed to it most likely to insure peace.

But peace did not follow. The condition of the Indians was at this time peculiarly critical, owing to the gradual extinction of the buffalo and the steady increase of western immigration. Many of the bands were depending upon the annuities due them by the recently made treaties to keep them from starvation. But there was delay in the Senate. The treaties made in the fall of 1867 were not ratified until after midsummer in 1868. The appropriations to carry these treaties into effect were consequently delayed. This the Indians could not understand. Moreover, many of them were in desperate need of food. In the case of some tribes there were other special grievances. Depredations followed, notably among the Cheyennes and Arapahoes, the rumors of which were grossly exaggerated. These depredations were regarded by the United States as a violation of the treaties not yet ratified, and preparations were made to punish the Indians. Thus another war was precipitated.*

---

* " My opinion is, in regard to the present Indian war, that the same could have been prevented, had the Government continued to keep up the supply of subsistence that had been furnished to them during the spring and early summer. They had gradually got weaned from their old habits to that extent that they depended upon the provisions which I issued to them, and consequently it was not necessary for them to scatter out in little bands all over the country for the purpose of finding game, thereby running risks of coming in contact with white men, and also being subjected to temptations when hungry ; but soon after the supplies were stopped. Had I been allowed to issue the arms and ammunition to them at the time promised, they would have been contented, from the fact of their having the means to procure game. But the failure of the Government to fulfill its promises in the latter respect naturally incensed some of the wilder spirits among them, and conse-

Meanwhile, October 9, 1868, the Indian Peace Commission had met at Chicago and drawn up a set of seven
resolutions,* repudiating much of their former work and
placing them in harmony with the War Department.
They then adjourned *sine die*, because, according to Colonel F. S. Tappan, "of their inability, for the want of
means, to do what had been promised the five thousand
or six thousand Indians now on the warpath."†

But a change was at hand, a change associated with
the name of President Grant and known as the Peace
Policy. It was officially inaugurated by the Indian
Appropriation Act of April 10, 1869.‡ Section IV of

---

quently the outrages committed on the Saline. * * * The Kiowa and
Comanche Indians up to the present time have been at peace, but I have no
doubt they will soon join the Cheyennes, and thus create a general Indian war. My reasons for believing that the Comanches and Kiowas
will, this late in the season, engage in this struggle, are that I do not see
how they can possibly do otherwise, in consequence of their having
been instructed some months since to assemble on the Arkansas for the
purpose of waiting to receive their agent and receive their annuities.
They have been waiting for months in a state of destitution, and no
agent or goods had made their appearance up to the latter part of last
month ; they are then told, without seeing their agent or receiving their
goods, to leave and go south immediately, to travel right through the
country where are troops in pursuit of hostile Indians, and with whom
it would be impossible to tell a Kiowa from a Cheyenne. The consequence will be that all the tribes of the upper Arkansas will before long
be engaged in hostilities." Letter from E. W. Wynkoop, United States
Indian Agent, to Colonel F. S. Tappan : Message and Documents, 1868-9,
Abridgment, 1016.

* See Report of the Indian Peace Commission to the President of
the United States : Messages and Documents, 1868-9 ; Abridgment,
1011.

† Letter from Colonel F. S. Tappan, Indian Peace Commissioner, to
Hon. N. G. Taylor, President of the Indian Peace Commission : *Ibid.*,
1016.

‡ U. S. Statutes at Large, XVI, 40.

this act provided, "that there be appropriated * * *
the sum of two millions of dollars, or so much thereof as
may be necessary, to enable the President to maintain
the peace among and with the various tribes, bands, and
parties of Indians, and to promote civilization among
said Indians, bring them, where practicable, upon reservations, relieve their necessities, and encourage their
efforts at self-support." This same act made provision
for the first feature of the peace policy. It authorized
the President to organize a board of not more than ten
commissioners, "to be selected by him from men emi-
nent for their intelligence and philanthropy," and "to
serve without pecuniary compensation," whose duty* it
should be "to exercise joint control with the Secretary
of the Interior over the disbursement of the above appropriation." Furthermore, $25,000 were appropriated "to
pay the necessary expenses of transportation, subsistence
and clerk hire of said commissioners while actually engaged in said service."†

The second feature‡ of the peace policy, and that most
characteristic of it, was the bringing of the various religious denominations of the country into active co-opera-
tion with the Government, by giving them the nomination
of Indian agents. The appointments were to be made
by the President and confirmed by the Senate. The
societies were to be held morally responsible for the
conduct of the appointees. At this time all superinten-

---

* For a more careful definition of the duties of this board, see Second
Annual Report, Board of Indian Commissioners, 1870, p. 100, Appendix
27.

† *Ibid.*, Preface.

‡ *Ibid.*, 4–5.

dents of Indian affairs and all Indian agents, with the
exception of those in Kansas and Nebraska, were officers
of the army, most of whom had been detailed for duty at
the close of the Civil War, in order to retrench expenses
and economize the public service.

Section XVIII of the Army Appropriation Act of July
15, 1870,* made it unlawful for any officer of the army
of the United States, on the active list, to hold a civil
office, either by election or appointment. On that day,
therefore, many Indian functionaries were relieved from
duty ; and it was proposed to fill their places with persons nominated by the various religious societies. This
principle was adopted to promote harmony between the
agents and missionaries and to purify the Indian service,
" by taking the nomination to the office of agent out of the
domain of politics and placing it where no motives but
those of disinterested benevolence could be presumed to
prevail."†

The third feature of the peace policy was the feeding
system, which provided for gathering the wilder tribes of
Indians upon reservations and supporting them until
taught to earn their own livelihood. The Government felt
that it was a question of either locating and feeding the
Indians or of fighting them. It chose the former course,
because this involved a less expenditure of money, " re-

---

* U. S. Statutes at Large, XVI, 319.

† Report of the Commissioner of Indian Affairs for 1872, p. 73. For
the year preceding the passage of the act of July 15, 1870, the Indian
superintendents and agents in Kansas and Nebraska had been appointed
by the President upon the recommendation of the two Societies of
Friends. The admirable working of this system led to its extension as
above indicated.

duced to the minimum the loss of life and property upon
our frontiers," and allowed "the freest development of
our settlements and railways possible under the circumstances."*

The feeding system was two-fold. On the one hand it
involved placing the Indians upon limited tracts of land ;
on the other, keeping them quiet by supporting them.
Neither of these ideas was absolutely new. The reservation system had existed in theory as far back as 1800,
and had been known under various forms and names
since then. The removal policy and the colonization
plan were simply modifications of it. But, as a feature
of the feeding system, it was of greater magnitude and
had two definite ends in view. It aimed to give the
Government some machinery of control over the Indians,
and to throw open a wide extent of country to the whites.
The policy of subsisting the Indians was adopted as the
cheapest and easiest way of buying off their hostility.
It, too, found a prototype as far back as 1800. On May
13 of that year an act† was passed authorizing the President to issue such rations as he should judge proper, and
as could be easily spared from the army provisions, to
Indians visiting the military posts or living in their reservations. Since then the friendship of the Indians had
been repeatedly purchased by the distribution of gifts.
But in 1870 the plan of subsisting the wilder tribes in
order to keep the peace became a definite feature of the
Indian policy.

---

* Report of the Commissioner of Indian Affairs for 1872, p. 4. This
report contains a most excellent presentation of the peace policy.

† U. S. Statutes at Large, II, 85.

The feeding system above outlined, and especially the reservation system, was, of course, a practical recognition of the dependence of the Indian tribes upon the United States Government. In theory, however, these tribes remained sovereign powers until denationalized by the act of March 3, 1871.* This provided that no tribe within the territory of the United States should be recognized as an independent nation with which the United States might treat.†

At first thought the passage of this act might seem to indicate a complete change in the national policy. In the hundreds of treaties which the Government had previously made with the Indians, they had been recognized as independent nations. Their tribal institutions had been left untouched, and they had been allowed to govern themselves as they chose. As a matter of fact, however, they had never been treated like sovereign powers. In the making of these very treaties the United States had used moral coercion, and frequently other and more effective means, to induce the tribes to yield to its terms. The relation of the Indian to the Government was in reality that of a ward under the care of a guardian. The power of the Indian agent had grown as the strength of the United States had increased and that of the Indians had decreased ; it had finally become practically absolute.‡

---

* Revised Statutes of the United States, Sect. 2079.

† This act further provided that "no obligation of any treaty lawfully made and ratified with any such Indian nation or tribe prior to March third, eighteen hundred and seventy-one," should be "invalidated or impaired." Revised Statutes of the U. S., Sect. 2079.

‡ Evolution of the Indian agent: Report of Commissioner of Indian Affairs for 1892, pp. 12-25.

The theory of Indian nationality was therefore a theory only,* and the act of March 3, 1871, was simply an outward recognition of an internal change which had already taken place.

The Feeding System was the term used to designate the policy of the United States toward the wilder tribes. Toward those more civilized it adopted a different attitude. These were to be taught to earn their own livelihood. They were to be transformed into farmers as rapidly as possible, were to receive land in severalty, and were to be furnished with agricultural implements. The Government proposed to spend as little money upon them as it could and still advance them in the arts of civilization.

The policy of the United States, in a nutshell, was this: The expenditures were to "be proportioned not to the good but to the ill deserts of the tribe;" hostile and potentially hostile tribes were to be supported in indolence in order to keep them quiet; well-disposed tribes were to be "only assisted to self-maintenance,"† since from them there was nothing to fear.‡ The ultimate object, however, with both was civilization.

The peace policy served its purpose well. It brought the Government into vital contact with nearly all the tribes living within the boundaries of the United States, and it furnished a system by which these tribes were, in a certain measure, controlled. The course of events during the decade between 1870 and 1880 served materially

---

* For the real status of the Indians, see Peters, V, 1.

† Report of the Commissioner of Indian Affairs for 1872, p. 4.

‡ Cf. appropriations for the wilder with those for the more civilized tribes. See Index of U. S. Statutes at Large.

to aid the designs of the Government. The object of the feeding system was to buy off the hostility of the Indians by supporting them. The success of this system depended, of course, upon the Indians' need of support. Hence scarcity of game must further the national policy. That this scarcity was every year becoming greater may be seen from the following quotation. Speaking of the buffalo, Colonel Dodge says :

"Their most prized feeding ground was the section of country between the South Platte and Arkansas Rivers, watered by the Republican, Smoky, Walnut, Pawnee, and other parallel and tributary streams, and generally known as the Republican country. Hundreds of thousands went south from here each winter but hundreds of thousands remained. It was the chosen home of the buffalo.

"In 1872 some enemy of the buffalo race discovered that their hides were merchantable, and could be sold in market for a goodly sum. The Union Pacific, Kansas Pacific, and Atchison, Topeka, and Santa Fé railroads soon swarmed with 'hard cases' from the East, each excited with the prospect of having a buffalo hunt that would pay. By wagon, on horseback, and a-foot, the pot hunters poured in, and soon the unfortunate buffalo was without a moment's peace or rest. Though hundreds of thousands of skins were sent to market, they scarcely indicated the slaughter. From want of skill in shooting, and want of knowledge in preserving the hides of those slain, on the part of these green hunters, one hide sent to market represented three, four, or even five dead buffalo.

"* * * In the fall of 1873 I went over the same ground. Where there were myriads of buffalo the year before, there were now myriads of carcasses. The air was foul with sickening stench, and the vast plain, which only a short twelvemonth before teemed with animal life, was now a dead, solitary, putrid desert."*

However unjust to the Indians this wholesale slaughter of buffalo may have been, there can be no doubt that it fell in admirably with the peace policy.† The Indians who were dependent upon the chase for a livelihood were forced to turn to the Government for help, and were obliged to accede to its demands. A machinery of control was thus established over them.

The incidental results of the peace policy were perhaps quite as important as those directly aimed at. The work of the Board of Indian Commissioners and the missionary societies co-operating with the Government acted like leaven upon the people of the country. Hitherto it had been almost impossible to interest the general public in the Indian question. In a country where legislation bears so close a relation to the popular demand, this was especially unfortunate. But beginning with the early seventies public interest in the welfare of the red race rapidly increased. Societies sprang up with the avowed purpose of agitating the Indian question and influencing the legislation of Congress. The decade from 1873 to 1883 witnessed the birth of the Boston Citizenship Committee, the Woman's National Indian Association, the

---

* Dodge, Plains of the Great West, 131–3.

† It must be remembered, however, that this same slaughter of buffalo often sent the Indians upon the warpath.

Indian Rights Association, and the Lake Mohonk Conference. Propagandic literature* was spread throughout the country and the seed sown whose fruit was the reform movement of the next decade.

Even on its weakest side, that of civilization, the peace policy was not an utter failure. The Indians, seated upon reservations and started upon an agricultural life, advanced ;† their progress was neither steady nor rapid, but was sufficient to encourage the friends of the Indians to look forward to ultimate citizenship for them. It was these friends, as yet largely represented by the societies above named, who began the agitation for "land, law, and education."

The agitation which brought about the reform movement arose, as before noted, in the seventies. It would be a difficult matter to separate the agitation from the movement proper, but the latter may be said to have begun about 1882. Its central principle was citizenship for the Indians, with all its attendant duties and privileges. These will be dwelt upon in treating the different phases of the movement.

The land question was primarily a question of allotment of lands in severalty and the granting of patents in fee simple. So long as the Indians should hold their land in common they must lack that incentive to work which comes from individual gain, and that education which accompanies individual responsibility. For many years community of property had been a hindrance to

---

* Much of this related to specific wrongs which the societies were endeavoring to right.

† See civilization statistics and the reports of the agents and farming superintendents: Reports of the Commissioner of Indian Affairs.

the civilization of the tribes. The friends of the Indians now urged that this **hindrance** be done away with **by** allotment in severalty.

As far back as **1839*** an act† had been passed which provided for individual allotments to the Brothertown Indians of Wisconsin. Subsequently, **by law** or treaty, allotment was extended to other tribes and bands,‡ provision being made in some cases **to confer the** rights of citizenship upon the allottees when they should have fulfilled certain conditions. But these acts were sporadic. The principle involved in them did not become a feature **of the** governmental policy until about 1858, and **even then did not** receive broad application.

A step forward was taken by the act **of** March 3, 1875,§ which extended the benefits of **the** Homestead Act of 1862‖ **to Indians,** and provided further that any homestead taken by an Indian should not be subject "to alienation or incumbrance ＊ ＊ ＊ for a period of five years from the date of the **patent** issued therefor."¶ It also provided that any Indian taking a homestead should not forfeit his right to tribal property. The defects of this act were **that it did** not provide for taking claims upon

---

* March 3.

† U. S. Statutes at Large, V, 349–51.

‡ "Notably the Ottawas and **Chippewas, the** Pottawatomies, the **Shawnees and** the Wyandottes." **Report of the** Commissioner of Indian Affairs for 1891, I, 40. The Commissioner goes on to say that in most cases the Indians sold their lands **as soon as** possible and squandered **what** little they received.

§ Supplement to the Revised Statutes of the U. S., I, 78.

‖ U. S. Statutes at Large, XII, 392–394.

¶ Supplement to the Revised Statutes, I, 78.

reservations, and that it made the time of inalienability too short.   In 1884 one thousand dollars was appropriated* to pay the fees incident to making the land entries, and subsequently other appropriations were made for the same purpose.   The benefits of the act were thus extended.

This brief outline of legislation will serve to show that in the case of individual tribes and Indians the Government had allotted lands in severalty, and, in some cases, had issued patents in fee simple.   The friends of the Indians now demanded that the principle involved in these measures be made of general application, and it was in response to this call that the Dawes Land in Severalty Bill was laid before Congress.   The following is an abstract of the same as given in the report of the Commissioner of Indian Affairs for 1887 : †

" The President may, in his discretion, have any Indian reservation or any part thereof surveyed or re-surveyed, and the lands of such reservation allotted in severalty to any Indian located thereon.

"The size of the allotments shall be : To each head of a family, one-quarter of a section ; to each single person over eighteen and each orphan under eighteen years of age, one-eighth of a section ; to each other single person born prior to the date of the Presidential order directing an allotment of lands upon the reserve, one-sixteenth of a section.

" If the reserve is too small to allow the giving of allotments as above, the size of allotments shall be reduced

---

* Supplement to Revised Statutes of the U. S., I, 450.

† Pp. iv-vi.

pro rata. If any treaty or act has provided for larger allotments on any reservation, the provisions of such treaty or act shall be observed. If the lands allotted are valuable only for grazing, the size of the allotments shall be doubled. If irrigation is necessary, the Secretary of the Interior may prescribe rules for a just distribution among the Indians of the water supply.

"Selections of allotments shall be made by Indians, heads of families selecting for their minor children, but agents shall select for orphans. The lands selected shall embrace the improvements made thereon by the respective Indians.

* * * * * * *

"If within four years after the President shall have directed allotments on a reservation any Indian belonging thereto shall have failed to make his selection, the agent, or if there is none a special agent, may make the selection for such Indian, and the tract so selected shall be allotted to him.

* * * * * * *

"Any Indian not residing on a reservation, or for whose tribe no reservation has been provided, may settle upon unappropriated Government land and have the same allotted and patented to him and his children.

* * * * * * *

"When the Secretary of the Interior shall have approved the allotment made, then patents for such lands, recorded in the General Land Office, shall be issued to the respective allottees, declaring that the United States will hold said lands in trust for their sole use and benefit for twenty-five years, and at the end of that time will convey them, without charge, to said allottees, or their heirs, in fee and free of all incumbrance ; the President, however, may in his discretion extend the period beyond twenty-five years.

" After patents have been delivered the laws of descent and partition of the State or Territory in which the lands are located shall apply to said lands ; the laws of Kansas applying to lands allotted to the Indian Territory.

" After lands have been allotted to all Indians of a tribe (or sooner if the President thinks best), the Secretary of the Interior may negotiate with that tribe for the sale of any of their unallotted lands, such negotiation to be subject to ratification by Congress.

" In case the lands are thus sold, the purchase money to be paid therefor by the United States shall be held in the United States Treasury in trust for that tribe, at three per cent. interest, which interest shall be subject to appropriation by Congress for the civilization of said tribe.

*   *   *   *   *   *   *

" After receiving his patent every allottee shall have the benefit of and be subject to the civil and criminal laws of the State or Territory in which he may reside ; and no Territory shall deny any Indian equal protection of law ; and every Indian born in the United States, who has received an allotment under this or any other law or treaty, or who has taken up his residence separate from a tribe and adopted the habits of civilized life, is declared a citizen of the United States ; but citizenship shall not impair any rights he may have in tribal property."*

---

* Report of the Commissioner of Indian Affairs for 1887, pp. iv-vi ; some of the less important provisions have been omitted in the above extract. For General Allotment Bill in full, see *ibid.*, 274-7.

Such were the provisions of the Dawes Land in Severalty Bill, a bill which was regarded by its supporters as marking the first step in the final solution of our Indian problem. Previous legislation had been in large measure tentative, had not been directed toward a definite end. True, it had aimed at the ultimate civilization of the Indians, but the measures adopted to bring about this civilization had lacked breadth and coherence.

The General Allotment Act was definite and comprehensive in scope. It made provision for the settlement of the Indian question. Tribal relations were to be dissolved and the Indians were to be made citizens of the United States as rapidly as possible, and at the end of twenty-five years were to be left to shift for themselves. The Government would then have done with them.

The natural corollary of the Dawes Bill was the ultimate break-up of the reservation system. This system had been in times past an unqualified necessity. It had served a two-fold purpose ; had protected the less warlike Indians from the murderous and rapacious whites ; had facilitated Government control over the more warlike. It has still a service to perform as a nursery for the less civilized Indians, until they can be fitted for contact with the world. But every allotment narrows its field, and ultimately it will have to go. As citizens, the Indians must take their places in the current of civilization and cannot expect to be separate from its swift movement.

The cession of surplus lands was, of course, the main factor in this break-up of reservations. In the year 1889–90 it was estimated that thirteen million acres of land were ceded to the Government, and, at the end of the year, there were agreements pending before Congress for the cession of four million five hundred thousand more.*

The sincerity of Congress in its attitude toward the new policy has been attested. When the Dawes Bill was put into practical working it was found that there were certain specific cases which it did not cover. Supplementary legislation was necessary, and, so far as the land question is concerned, Congress has sought to supply it.†

But the land question does not stand by itself. It is indissolubly connected with law and education. The Indians are citizens only in name if not protected by United States courts and educated by United States schools. Hence the second feature of the reform movement was law.

It is not proposed to treat at all fully the past or present political status of the Indians under the United States Government. Such a treatment would demand more time and space than can be given it here ; but a few generalizations may be of use. In the early days of our Republic the autonomy of the various tribes was recognized in theory and in fact. The first "agents" appointed by President Washington were addressed as "commissioners plenipotentiary for negotiating and con-

---

* Report of Commissioner of Indian Affairs for 1890, xxxviii.

† The act of February 28, 1891, amended the General Allotment Act so as to provide for the allotment of the same quantity of land to each member of the tribe regardless of the age or status of the allottee. See U. S. Statutes at Large, xxvi, 794.

Numerous other acts were passed, many of them pertaining only to certain tribes.

cluding treaties of peace with the independent tribes or
nations of Indians * * * south of the Ohio River."*
As our frontiers were pushed westward, and we came
into more vital contact with the red men, it became
necessary, for the sake of peace, to obtain some control
over them ; and to this end the powers of the agents were
gradually increased, still however mainly in the direction
of regulating intercourse between the whites and the
Indians.

Infringement upon tribal autonomy began with the act
of June 30, 1834.† The authority of the governmental
officials was enlarged to extend over the Indians and over
the Indian country. Among other things this act gave
the agent the power "to procure the arrest and trial of
all Indians accused of committing any crime, offense, or
misdemeanor." The act of March 3, 1847,‡ and that of
March 27, 1854,§ still further extended the powers of the
agent. These encroachments upon tribal sovereignty
were made in the interests of peace and the security of
our frontiers. It was not the purpose to weaken tribal
law, but this result inevitably followed. Thus the Indians
were practically under no restraint but the arbitrary
rule of the agent, and they possessed absolutely no redress
for grievances. It was natural, therefore, that the agitation which began with the peace policy should concern
itself with the question of law.

The appointment of Indian police was the direct out-

---

* Letter of Washington : Report of Commissioner of Indian Affairs
for 1892, p. 14.

† U. S. Statutes at Large, IV, 732.

‡ Ibid., IX, 203.

§ Ibid., X, 270.

come of this agitation. In the Appropriation Act of May
27, 1878,* Congress authorized the appointment of fifty
officers and four hundred and thirty privates to maintain
order and prohibit illegal traffic on the reservations. A
force was immediately organized† at thirty different
agencies, and the Indian police showed themselves worthy
of the trust reposed in them. Their duties took a wider
range than was at first anticipated. They made themselves active in suppressing disorder and violence and in
preventing trespass and robbery on the part of lawless
whites.

The next step in the direction of law was the establishment of the courts of Indian offenses. Upon the request
of the Secretary of the Interior the Commissioner of
Indian Affairs formulated certain rules for the abolition
of the sun-dance, the scalp-dance, polygamy, and other
barbarous practices. In accordance with these rules,
courts were organized on the various reservations, each
consisting of three Indian judges appointed by the Indian
Office upon the nomination of the agent, and serving for
one year, subject, however, to removal at any time.
These courts held regular bi-monthly sessions. Some
difficulties were at first experienced in their organization,
largely because no provision had been made to recom-
pense the judges; but, once organized, they did good
work. The penalties imposed were fines, imprisonment,
hard labor, and forfeiture of rations. The courts were

---

* Report of the Commissioner of Indian Affairs for 1878, p. 188.

† One difficulty in the organization of these forces was the small sal-
ary, officers receiving only eight dollars and privates five dollars a
month. It was not easy to find competent men who would serve for such
sums.

established in 1883, but were not recognized by law until 1888, when Congress appropriated five thousand dollars for the compensation of Indian judges.*

The third step toward law was the Indian Crimes Act,† passed March 3, 1885. It provided that all Indians committing " murder, manslaughter, rape, assault with intent to kill, arson, burglary, and larceny, within any Territory of the United States, and either within or without an Indian reservation," should be subject therefor to the laws of such Territory relating to said crimes ; and that Indians committing the enumerated crimes within the boundaries of a State should be tried by United States courts. The defect of this act lay in the failure to provide for the reimbursement of the Territories. They were unwilling to bear the cost of trying the Indians because they derived no revenue from them.

The three measures here reviewed were crude attempts to furnish the Indians with law. They were good as far as they went, but they accomplished little more than the maintenance of order through the arbitrary power of the agent. Further legislation was needed, and this need was accentuated, at the same time that its satisfaction was made more difficult, by the passage of the General Allotment Bill. The state of the case was this : omitting the tribes maintaining an advanced government of their own, those so unenlightened or so situated as to be unable to comprehend the advantages of civilization, and those still nomadic and not yet under the charge of any agent—omitting these, the Indians might roughly be

---

* Act of June 29, 1888.   See U. S. Statutes at Large, xxv, 233.

† *Ibid.*, xxiii, 385.

divided into two classes. The first class included those already or soon to become citizens of the United States ; the second, those who must undergo a tutelage more or less long before the President should deem them ready for the action of the Land in Severalty Bill. Citizenship would extend over the first class the jurisdiction of the courts of the States and Territories in which the members respectively resided ; but these States and Territories provided no machinery for the administration of law upon the reservations. This need would, of course, be met with the sale of the surplus land and its occupation by white settlers. In the meantime, however, the need must continue to exist unless satisfaction could be provided in another way. The second class of Indians, those who must remain for some years longer under the guardianship of the United States, were eventually to become citizens. To fit them for the duties and privileges which would then be theirs, they ought gradually to be made familiar with the simpler forms of legal procedure ; and for this courts were necessary.

It was a question of meeting the needs of one or both of these classes. After a careful consideration of the subject, Commissioner Morgan decided that the utmost that could be done at present was to help the non-citizen Indians by extending the jurisdiction of the courts of Indian offenses. With this end in view he enlarged and modified the regulations under which the courts were established. Sufficient time has not elapsed to test the working of the new rules.*

The vital connection which education bears to the rest

---

* Report of the Commissioner of Indian Affairs for 1892, pp. 27-31.

of the reform movement is apparent on the surface.
Citizenship does not rightfully belong to the incapable
and the unlettered. The Indians must be made worthy
of their new dignity, and one means to this end is to be
found in an effective school system.

Education had been theoretically a part of the civilization policy of the Government for many years. As far
back as March 3, 1819, Congress had passed an act*
appropriating ten thousand dollars annually for the
payment of suitable persons to instruct the Indians in
agriculture, and to teach their children reading, writing,
and arithmetic. February 27 of that same year the
United States had agreed to sell certain lands belonging to the Cherokee Indians for the purpose of raising a
fund to educate their youth.† Subsequently, agreements
had been made with numerous tribes to set aside a portion of their annuities for the support of schools. In
many of the treaties made by the Peace Commission in
1868, the Indians had pledged themselves to send all
their children between the ages of six and sixteen to
school, and the United States had promised to erect a
school-house and employ a teacher for every thirty who
should attend.‡

But it was not until 1876 that Indian education, as
now understood, was begun by the Government. In that
year, in addition to the amounts due the various tribes
by treaty for educational purposes, Congress appropriated
twenty thousand dollars for the support of Indian

* U. S. Statutes at Large, III, 516.

† American State Papers, Indian Affairs, II, 188.

‡ See U. S. Statutes at Large, xv.

schools. In 1879 an act was passed, authorizing the
Secretary of War "to detail an officer of the army * *
* for special duty with reference to Indian education."*
In 1882 the office of Inspector of Schools† was created,
but the incumbent was invested with no powers.‡ Meanwhile the annual appropriations steadily increased, passing in 1886 the million point.

The passage of the Land in Severalty Bill had a direct
bearing upon the education question. In withholding
from the Indians for twenty-five years the power to
alienate their lands, it left them in a state of "quasi-
independence"; and, in exempting their lands from
taxation for the same length of time, it practically ex-
cluded their children from public schools. It thus became
the duty of the Government to make educational provision
for these children, and recent legislation would seem to
indicate that Congress views the matter in the same
light. The duties of the Superintendent of Indian
Schools have been broadened ; § compulsory education

---

* Report of Commissioner of Indian Affairs for 1879, p. 189.

† Report of Commissioner of Indian Affairs for 1882, p. 196.

‡ "The first Superintendent died in 1885, and his successor says of
him that he was esteemed an able and excellent man, ' but at the time
of his death he had not determined the functions of his office.' His successor was appointed in the following May, and when he made his
report in November, 1885, had found out that ' the duties of the office
were suggested by its title, but not defined by law.' When he resigned
his office to take another position, after a year's faithful effort to find out
what these duties were, he was decidedly of the opinion that they consisted largely of bearing responsibility before the public for acts which
he had no power to originate or determine." Eighteenth Annual Report
of the Board of Indian Commissioners, 1886, p. 65.

§ See U. S. Statutes at Large, xxiv, 464.

has been adopted ;* Superintendents, Assistant Superintendents, and teachers have been put on the classified
list of the Civil Service ;† last, but not least, the annual
appropriations have been exceedingly generous.

The present educational policy began, as before said,
about twenty years ago. Its rapid growth may be
seen from a comparison of the appropriations of 1876
and 1892, that of the latter year being nearly one hundred and fifteen times as large as that of the former.‡
The Government has not itself, however, supervised the
expenditure of all this money. It has given a portion of
it into the hands of religious bodies for the conduct of
their schools.§ In the beginning this course was doubtless wise. But with the flight of time has come a growing sentiment that this union of church and State is
contrary to the spirit of our institutions and in direct
violation to the first amendment of our Constitution,
which provides that "Congress shall make no laws
respecting an establishment of religion or prohibiting
the free exercise thereof."‖ It has been alleged also that
a premium is being put upon "the use of ecclesiastical
power for political purposes in the shaping of legislation."¶ This sentiment was re-enforced by the refusal of

---

* See U. S. Statutes at Large, xxvi, 1014.

† See Report of the Commissioner of Indian Affairs for 1891, I,
156–8. The machinery necessary to enforce these rules is still lacking.

‡ The appropriations reached their maximum in 1892. Those for
1893 and 1894 have been less. See Report of the Commissioner of Indian Affairs for 1894, p. 9.

§ This feature of the educational policy was adopted in 1819. See
American State Papers, Indian Affairs, II, 200–1, 272, 275–7.

‖ Report of the Board of Indian Commissioners for 1890, p. 92.

¶ *Ibid.*, 93–4.

the Bureau of Catholic Missions to submit to Government regulations imposed alike upon contract and Government schools. The consequent agitation resulted in a decrease of the amount appropriated to contract schools in 1893, and in the passage of an act in 1894, directing the Secretary of the Interior " to inquire into and investigate the propriety of discontinuing contract schools."* This would seem to point to the ultimate assumption by Government of the entire control of Indian education.

Such are the lines along which the reform movement is working. Sufficient time has not yet elapsed to justify a prediction as to its final results, but these will be determined largely during the next few years. Now, if ever, the Indians need the friends who have served them so well during the last two decades. The Land in Severalty Bill is open to evils which must be carefully guarded against. Most notable among these are throwing open the reservations to allotment before the Indians are ready for it, and settling the Indians upon poor lands. The first is caused by the rapacity of the whites for surplus lands ; and the second, by their desire that these lands shall be of the best.† Manifestly the preventive of these evils lies in a pure administration of our Indian service. The Government officers, from the highest to the lowest, must be men of integrity and ability, and must not be removed for political reasons. The spoils system must be entirely abandoned. A step in this direction was taken by President Harrison, who, by executive order,

---

* **Twelfth Annual Report** of the Executive Committee of the Indian **Rights Association, 8.**

† See Twelfth Annual Report **of the** Executive Committee of **the** Indian Rights Association, 37-38.

April 13, 1891, extended the Civil Service rules so as to embrace the appointments of Superintendents, Assistant Superintendents, physicians, teachers, and matrons. The welfare of the Indians demands a further extension of these rules. The agents are as yet selected without any guarantee as to their integrity or fitness for the positions which they are to occupy ; and these agents are, and must remain for some time, most important factors in the development of the Indians, and upon them largely depends the preparation of these Indians for citizenship.

Finally, the thorough carrying out of the reform movement demands a comprehensive system* of education. Enough schools must be provided to accommodate all the Indian youth, and of such a character as to make it possible to merge them ultimately in our public school system.† We have attempted a final solution of the Indian question. The character of the solution, however, is still a problem. It may be that after all we are forcing citizenship upon the Indians before they are ready for it. Even at this late date a change of policy may be necessary. It is the duty of the American people, as represented by Congress, to study the results of the present policy so carefully that their future legislation shall redound to the welfare of the Indians and to the honor of the Republic.

---

* For an outline of such a system, see T. J. Morgan's Indian Education.

† The Indian Office is making an effort in this direction by offering the public schools of the States ten dollars a quarter for every Indian child within their limits who shall attend.

CHAPTER II.

THE SIOUX FROM 1803 TO 1850.

It was in the year 1803, during the presidency of Jefferson, that the United States purchased the Louisiana Territory from France. It was a country of vast extent, larger in area than the original thirteen colonies, and of great resources, but as yet little known. That portions of it abounded in rich fur-bearing animals was evidenced by the lucrative trade which the English carried on with the natives ; and it was Jefferson's desire to turn this trade into American channels which prompted the Lewis and Clark expeditions of the years 1804 to 1806.* He wished to open a field to the private American trader whom the Government trading-houses had dislodged east of the Mississippi ; and with this end in view he urged the exploration of the Missouri to its source and the search for an overland route to the Pacific. The advance in the geographical knowledge of our continent was regarded as purely incidental, as "an additional gratification."†

The expedition was made, and the records of it furnish us with our first reliable information concerning the location of the Sioux tribes. It will be necessary to pause here for a moment to draw the distinction between the terms Siouan and Sioux. Siouan is an adjective derived from the word Sioux and used to denote the entire lin-

---

* See Jefferson's Message of January 18, 1803: Amer. State Papers, Ind. Affs., I, 684.

† American State Papers, Ind. Affs., I, 685.

guistic stock of which the Sioux, or more **properly the** Dakotas, are the most important division. **Sioux is "a corruption** of the Algonkin word *nadowe-ssi-wag*, 'the snake-like ones'. * * * The **term** 'Dahcota' (Dakota) was correctly applied **by Gallatin** to the Dakota **tribes** proper as distinguished **from the** other members of the linguistic family **who are not Dakotas in a** tribal sense."*

Lewis and **Clark left St. Louis May 14, 1804, and** ascended the Missouri **river to its source, at the same** time exploring much of the surrounding country. **They** then **crossed** the Rocky Mountains, and followed **the Columbia** river to the Pacific Ocean, returning **to St.** Louis after an absence of two years and four **months.** During this expedition **they visited** the various Sioux tribes, obtained **as much** information about them as they could **under** the circumstances, and located them as **definitely as was possible with** a roving people. According to Lewis and Clark, the Sioux were divided into ten bands, and, to **quote** the words of these explorers, were located as follows :

" **First, Yanktons.** This tribe inhabits the Sioux, Des Moines, and Jacques rivers, and **numbers about two hun-**dred warriors.

" Second, Tetons of the Burnt Woods. * * * This tribe numbers about three hundred men, **who** rove on both sides of the Missouri, White, **and Teton** rivers.

"Third, Tetons Okandandas (Ogallalas), a tribe consisting of about **one** hundred and fifty men, who inhabit both sides of the Missouri below the Cheyenne river.

---

* **Report of the** Bureau of Ethnology, 1885–6, 111–112.

"Fourth, Tetons Minnakenozzo (Minneconjou), a nation inhabiting both sides of the Missouri above the Cheyenne river, and containing about two hundred and fifty men.

"Fifth, Tetons Saone.   These inhabit both sides of the Missouri below the Warreconne river, and consist of about three hundred men.

"Sixth, Yanktons of the   *   *   *   Plains, or Big Devils, who rove on the heads of the Sioux, Jacques, and Red rivers ; the most numerous of all the tribes, numbering about five hundred men.

"Seventh, Wahpatone, * * * a nation residing on the St. Peter's, just above the mouth of that river, numbering two hundred men.

"Eighth, Mindawarcarton (Mdewakantonwan). * * * These possess the original seat of the Sioux, and are properly so denominated.   They rove on both sides of the Mississippi about the falls of St. Anthony, and consist of three hundred men.

"Ninth, The Wahpatoota (Wahpekute). * * * This nation inhabits both sides of the river St. Peter's, below Yellow-wood river, amounting to about one hundred and fifty men.

"Tenth, Sistasoone (Sisseton).   This nation numbers two hundred men, who reside at the head of St. Peter's."*

The aggregate number of souls in these bands was about nine thousand three hundred.   This was, however, only approximate ; for it must be remembered that they were roving bands, moving hither and thither as the exigencies of the hunt or trade might require.   The Statistical View of 1806 says that much of the land belonging

---

* Coues' Lewis and Clark Expedition, I, 97–102.

to the Sioux was fertile, and a large part of it well tim-
bered and watered. The Mdewakantonwans, however, were
the only band that cultivated corn, etc.; and even these
could not properly be termed a stationary people. The
Sissetons, living in a country abounding in valuable fur-
bearing animals, such as the beaver, otter, and martin,
purchased more merchandise in proportion to their numbers than any other neighboring tribe ; and disposed of
a large part of this merchandise in their trade with the
Tetons. As a rule, these tribes, together with the Wahpekute and Wahpeton, their neighbors, treated their
traders well.*

Certainly as much could not be said of the Tetons,
" the pirates of the Missouri." These, says Clark, " rely-
ing on a regular supply of merchandise through the
channel of the river St. Peter's, * * * view with
contempt the merchants of the Missouri, whom they
never fail to plunder when in their power."† And this,
he thought, they would continue to do until, in his own
words, " such measures are pursued by our Government
as will make them feel a dependence on its will for their
supply of merchandise."‡

The Yanktons, says Lewis, " are the best disposed
Sioux who rove on the banks of the Missouri, and these
even will not suffer any trader to ascend the river, if
they can possibly avoid it ; they have heretofore, invari-

---

* Lewis' Statistical View: Coues' Lewis and Clark Expedition, I,
99–100, note.

† Lewis' Statistical View, 1806: Coues' Lewis and Clark Expedition, I, 128, note 67.

‡ Lewis' Statistical View, 1806: Coues' Lewis and Clark Expedition,
I, 128, note 67.

ably, arrested the progress of all those they have met with, and generally compelled them to trade at the prices, nearly, which they themselves think proper to fix on their merchandise. * * * Their trade, if well regulated, might be rendered extremely valuable."* This band was independent of the other Sioux bands, as, indeed, each was of the others.

Such are the important facts concerning the Sioux in the years 1805–6. On the whole, Lewis and Clark's classification is remarkably close to that recently made by Major J. W. Powell, Director of the Bureau of Ethnology.† Several bands of Tetons are omitted in the former, but, under the circumstances, such a discrepancy is not surprising.

---

* Coues' Lewis and Clark Expedition, I, 94, footnote 8. Quoted from Statistical View, London ed., 1807, p. 18.

† Major J. W. Powell's classification is as follows:

A. Sontee: including Mdewakantonwan and Wahpekute. [Lewis and Clark's eighth and ninth tribes.]
B. Sisseton. [Lewis and Clark's tenth tribe.]
C. Wahpeton. [Lewis and Clark's seventh tribe.]
D. Yankton. [Lewis and Clark's first tribe.]
E. Yanktonnais. [Lewis and Clark's sixth tribe.]
F. Teton.
    (a) Brulé. [Lewis and Clark's second tribe.]
    (b) Sans Arcs.
    (c) Blackfeet.
    (d) Minneconjou. [Lewis and Clark's fourth tribe.]
    (e) Two Kettles.
    (f) Ogallala. [Lewis and Clark's third tribe.]
    (g) Uncpapa.

Report of the Bureau of Ethnology for 1885–6, 114–15.

There has been much discussion concerning Lewis and Clark's fifth tribe. Coues says the balance of evidence is in favor of referring it to the Yanktonnais: Coues' Lewis and Clark Expedition, I, 101, note 10.

In the year 1805 Captain Zebulon M. Pike was com-
missioned by the War Department to explore the sources
of the Mississippi and " the internal parts of Louisiana."*
In his report of this expedition we find some interesting
comments on the fur trade. Mr. Jay's treaty of 1794†
had given British subjects the right to trade with Indians on American soil, but had not " exempted them
from paying the duties, obtaining licenses, and subscrib-
ing unto all the rules and restrictions of our laws."‡
They had accepted the privilege, but not the obligations
accompanying it. As a result they were able to under-
sell our traders ; and, indeed, had quite driven them
from the field. Lieutenant Pike laid the matter before
the Northwest Company, and obtained from it a promise
to observe our regulations in the future. This advantage
was followed in 1809 by the organization of the American
Fur Company, which in 1811 was consolidated with the
Mackinaw Company and formed the Southwest Company. But in 1812 the war broke out, and the trade of
the Southwest Company was ruined. The company re-
appeared, however, in 1816, the same year in which
Congress passed a law§ prohibiting foreigners from carrying on the fur trade within the territories of the United

---

* Captain Pike's classification and location of the Sioux tribes agrees
substantially with that made by Lewis and Clark. His judgment of
their numbers is greater and his conception of their morality higher ;
but these are points upon which individual explorers might well differ,
depending upon the extent and thoroughness of the exploration, the
temper of the natives at the time and their reception of the explorers.

† See Treaties and Conventions, 380-1.

‡ Pike's Expedition, Appendix to Part I, 14.

§ U. S. Statutes at Large, III, 332.

States. This was aimed at the English and was designed to end their influence over our Indian tribes. But it was soon found that foreign clerks, interpreters, and boatmen could not be dispensed with ; and, in the summer of 1816, the Secretary of the Treasury issued orders to Indian agents to license foreigners in these capacities " on their giving bond with large penalties for good conduct in the Indian country."* British traders eagerly seized this opportunity, passed the American agencies in the guise of clerks and interpreters, and, once in the country, took possession of the goods which had made their way through the lines as the property of an American, whose employee the British trader had presumably been.† The English, therefore, continued to hold a monopoly of the fur trade for some years longer ; and this despite the fact that in 1814 the Government had " provided for locating trading posts " at Green Bay and Prairie du Chien, and in 1816 had sent garrisons there.‡ Here, as elsewhere, the Government trading-houses proved a failure. They neither attached the Indians to the United States, nor counteracted the influence of the British trader. During these years, therefore, the Sioux were unaffected by the national policy.

In the war of 1812 the Indians of the Northwest had, for the most part, sided with Great Britain ; and, at the close of the war, treaties were made between the United

---

* Wis. Hist. Colls., II, 103.

† See Wis. Hist. Colls., II, 103 ; Minn. Hist. Colls., V, 9 ; Turner, Character and Influence of Indian Trade in Wisconsin, 57-8. For the attitude of the English toward these posts, as affecting their relations with the Indians, see Mich. Pioneer Colls., XVI, 76 ff.

‡ Turner, Character and Influence of Indian Trade in Wisconsin, 58.

States and the various tribes for the purpose of re-estab-
lishing peace and friendship.   These treaties read as
follows :

"Article 1.   Every injury, or act of hostility, committed by one or either of the contracting parties against
the other, shall be mutually forgiven and forgot.

"Art. 2.   There shall be perpetual peace and friendship between all the citizens of the United States of
America and all the individuals composing the said
—— tribe ; and the friendly relations that existed between
them before the war shall be, and the same are hereby,
renewed.

"Art. 3.   The undersigned chiefs and warriors, for
themselves and their said tribe, do hereby acknowledge
themselves and their aforesaid tribe to be under the
protection of the United States of America, and of no
other nation, power, or sovereign whatsoever."*

During the years 1815 and 1816 five such treaties were
made with the Sioux ; one with the "Teetons,"† one with
the " Sioux of the Lakes "‡ (Mdewakantonwan), one with
the "Sioux of the river St. Peter's "§ (Wahpeton), one
with the " Yanctons,"‖ and one with the " Siouxs of the
Leaf, the Siouxs of the Broad Leaf, and the Siouxs
who shoot in the Pine Tops "¶ (probably Wahpekute).

From this time until 1825 the Government had but
slight dealings with these bands.   The United States

---

* U. S. Statutes at Large, VII, 125.

† *Ibid.*

‡ *Ibid.*, 126.

§ *Ibid.*, 127.

‖ *Ibid.*, 128.

¶ *Ibid.*, 143.

had not yet extended its frontiers to their territory, and there were no critical conditions calling for legislation. It was the almost continuous intertribal warfare between the Sioux and their inveterate enemies, the Chippewas, and the wars between the Sioux, Sacs and Foxes, and Ioways, which next called the attention of the United States to the western Indians. These constant feuds interrupted trade and endangered the lives of those citizens living in this part of the country. Sound polity, therefore, and humanitarian motives regarding the welfare of the Indians prompted the Government to attempt mediation. Accordingly, commissioners were sent to Prairie du Chien, and August 19, 1825, a treaty was made " with the Sioux and Chippewa, Sacs and Fox, Manominie, Ioway, Sioux, Winnebago, and a portion of the Ottawa, Chippewa, and Potawattomie tribes."*

By this treaty boundaries† were established between the tribes, and perpetual peace declared between those that had been at war.

During this same year three other treaties were made with the Sioux‡ to perpetuate friendship with them and to remove all future dissention concerning trade. In these treaties the various bands promised to protect the persons and property of United States traders and agents,

---

* U. S. Statutes at Large, VII, 272 ff. The Sioux were represented by the "Wahpetong," "Sussitong," "Wappacoota," "Medawakanton" and "Yancton" tribes.

† These boundary lines were not complete because some of the tribes interested were absent from the council.

‡ One with the "Teton, Yanctons, and Yanctonies bands:" U. S. Statutes at Large, VII, 250 ; one with the "Siouna and Ogallala tribes:" ibid., 252 ; one with the "Hunkpapas band:" ibid., 257.

to give safe conduct to persons legally authorized by the
United States to pass through their country, and to
apprehend and deliver to United States authorities foreigners not so authorized. There were other provisions
of minor importance concerning points which, if not
made clear, might cause future trouble.*

The treaty of Prairie du Chien, which had been made
in the hope of promoting peace between the warring
bands of Indians, did not accomplish its object. In the
report of the Commissioner of Indian Affairs for 1829–30,
we read that the Sioux and Sacs and Foxes are still
fighting each other,† and that they will, it is presumed,
continue to do so "until some one or other of the tribes
shall become too reduced and feeble to carry on the war,
when it will be lost as a separate power."‡ Meanwhile,
however, the United States again attempted mediation,
and this led to the treaty of July 15, 1830. According to
Article I of this treaty, the Indians relinquished a certain
tract of land between the Missouri and Demoine rivers.
This tract was to be assigned or allotted under the direction of the President of the United States to the tribes
then living thereon, or to such other tribes as the President might locate thereon for hunting or other purposes.
In consideration of this cession the United States agreed
to pay the various tribes certain annuities for ten years,§

---

* See U. S. Statutes at Large, VII, 253, Art. 5. This article provided for the punishment of individuals for injuries done the Indians,
and for the recovery of stolen property or indemnification therefor.

† For a graphic account of one of these Indian massacres, see Wis.
Hist. Colls., IX, 323 ff.

‡ Niles Register, XXXVII, 363.

§ To the Sioux of the Mississippi, two thousand dollars. To the
Yankton and Santee bands, three thousand dollars. To the Mdewakan-

and to spend annually for the same number of years
three thousand dollars in educating their children.   The
Yankton and Santee bands of Sioux were not represented
. at the council at which these articles were drawn up, but
signed the treaty some seven months later.   That the
provisions of this treaty were not understood by all the
Indian tribes party to it, is demonstrated by the trouble
which arose when the President assigned the ceded tract
of land to the Winnebagoes.   The Sioux then asserted
that, at the council, one of the United States Commissioners had explained to them that this was to be neutral
territory, held in trust by the United States for the tribes
party to the treaty by which it had been ceded.*   The
words of Article I, however, bore out the United States,
and the Sioux finally yielded.

During the next few years little was heard of the Sioux.
They were scarcely mentioned at all in the reports of the
Commissioner of Indian Affairs except in connection
with the annuities due them by the treaty of 1830.   The
United States had grown hardened to the intertribal warfare upon its northwestern frontier, a warfare which apparently it was powerless to stop ; and the Sioux were
left to themselves.

It was in behalf of the State of Missouri that the Gov-

----

tonwan, Wahpekute, Wahpeton, and Sisseton bands of Sioux, "one
blacksmith at the expense of the United States, and the necessary
tools ; also instruments for agricultural purposes, and iron and steel to
the amount of seven hundred dollars."   To the Yankton and Santee
bands of Sioux, "one blacksmith at the expense of the United States,
and the necessary tools, also instruments for agricultural purposes to the
amount of four hundred dollars."   U. S. Statutes at Large, VII, 329.

* See Report of the Commissioner of Indian Affairs for 1836–7 : Ex.
Docs., 24th Cong., 2nd Sess., Vol. I, 369–70.

ernment next approached them. By the treaty of Prairie
du Chien in 1830, the Indians, as before said, ceded a
certain tract of land with the understanding that it was
to be assigned to the tribes then living thereon, or to be
located thereon in the future by the President. A portion of this tract lay between the western boundary of
Missouri and the Missouri river.* This the citizens of
the State were naturally anxious to possess, and the Fed-
eral Government was induced to treat with the Indians
for its cession. Conventions were held with the various
tribes in the fall of 1836, and the land purchased of them.†
The Sioux sold their right for $1,950, Wabashaw's tribe
receiving $400,‡ the Yankton and Santee bands $1,000,§
the Wahpekute, Sisseton, and Upper Mdewakantonwan
tribes $550.‖

This was the first of a series of cessions. The second
was made in the year 1837, and this time the motives
which prompted the United States to treat were of national importance. Negotiations were begun in pursu-
ance of the central principle of the removal policy, the
policy of buying up all the Indian lands in the States and
Territories, and massing the Indians on the west side of the
Mississippi. Deputations of chiefs were invited to Washington to impress them with the strength of our nation,

---

* See U. S. Statutes at Large, VII, 328-9.

† There were three separate treaties with the Sioux.

‡ U. S. Statutes at Large, VII, 510-11.

§ Ibid., 525.

‖ Ibid., 527. The next year the Yanktons sold their right to the entire tract of land ceded by the various tribes to the Government in 1830,
with the provision that it should remain Indian country. This treaty of
October 21, 1837, with the Yanktons has been omitted from the text for
the sake of simplification. See U. S. Statutes at Large, VII, 542-3.

and to make them sensible of the advantages which flow from civilization. It was during this visit that the Mdewakantonwan Sioux ceded to the United States all their lands "east of the Mississippi river and all their islands in the said river."* The United States, on its part, promised to invest the sum of $300,000 in safe State stocks, and to pay the Indians "annually, forever," an interest of five per cent. thereon ; to distribute $110,000 among the mixed bloods ; to apply $90,000 to the payment of the just debts of the tribe ; to pay $10,000 annually for twenty years to the chiefs and braves ; to expend $8,250 annually for twenty years "in the purchase of medicines, agricultural implements and stock and for the support of a physician, farmers and blacksmiths ;" to expend $5,500 annually for twenty years in the purchase of provisions ; to supply the Indians as soon as possible, to an amount not exceeding $10,000, "with agricultural implements, mechanics' tools, cattle and such other articles" as might be useful to them ; to deliver $6,000 in goods to the chiefs and braves.

If we may judge from the above provisions, an attempt was to be made to start the Mdewakantonwans upon an agricultural life. They had subsisted hitherto chiefly by the hunt, although as far back as 1805 they had been known to raise small quantities of corn and beans. But dependence upon the hunt was becoming somewhat precarious. The results of the long continued depredations of the British half-breeds, who crossed the border and killed great numbers of buffalo,† were beginning to be

---

* U. S. Statutes at Large, VII, 538.

† " The British half-breeds of the North Red river still continue their annual incursions upon the hunting grounds of the Sioux within our ter-

felt.   Other game, too, was becoming scarce and the trade
in furs had decreased.   The annuities were therefore
very welcome to the Mdewakantonwans.   But they showed
little inclination to settle down to agriculture.   It would
have been strange indeed if they had shown any.   It
would have meant the laying aside of instincts and
habits, and the adoption of an entirely new mode of life.
Moreover, the United States was by no means prompt
in providing agricultural implements, tools, and cattle.
The backwardness of the Mdewakantonwans in taking
hold of farming seems, therefore, most natural, and the
discouragement of the agent a little unreasonable.   At
this time, too, the whisky traffic was exerting a most
demoralizing influence over the Indians.   The liquor was
introduced largely by factors of the Hudson's Bay Company, though our own traders were not without fault.
Suffering from scarcity of game, demoralized by whisky,
and harassed by their fierce enemies, the Chippewas, the
Sioux had a sorry time of it.   No wonder the Commissioner wrote in 1847 that there was a strong desire among

---

ritory, and slaughter large numbers of buffalo, the meat of which is
dried, and used for the subsistence of the traders connected with the
Hudson's Bay Company, and also kill other animals valuable for their
furs.   * * *   These incursions have led to quarrels and disputes between them and the Sioux, some of which are said to have been attended with fatal consequences.   The British half-breeds complained of are
represented as numerous, warlike, and well armed, and consequently
come into our territory prepared to resist any attempt on the part of the
Sioux to drive them away." Report of Commissioner of Indian Affairs,
1845–6: Sen. Ex. Docs., 2nd Sess., 28th Cong., I, 454.

The United States sent a detachment of dragoons in 1845 to inform
these half breeds that they would not be allowed to hunt within our territories, but this order had little effect.

them to increase their **annuities and** that land was probably purchasable.*

Such **is a brief** outline of the history of the Sioux from
1803 to 1850. Thus far they had been a factor of com-
paratively slight importance in the determination of the
governmerital policy, and had been little affected by it.
Placed on the frontiers **of** the United States, and remote
from civilized communities of any **size, they** had been
left free to live as they chose, **the Government** paying
little heed to them except as it found occasion to make
treaties with the various tribes and bands. Up to this
time no accurate estimate had been made of their numbers, **and only a few tribes** had **been at all** definitely located. **With the** great body of the Sioux roaming over the
plains **of the** Missouri the Government had had no relations whatever,† and its hold upon even the **Sioux** of the
Mississippi‡ was very loose. An attempt, as we have
seen, had been made to start the Mdewakantonwans upon
an agricultural **life. But** that the Government was not
sanguine as to the result of this attempt may be seen
from these words of the Commissioner of Indian Affairs
in 1848 : **"Of the Sioux it is not** probable that many
will remain **for** any considerable period in the Mississippi
regions ; wild and untameable and scattered **over** an immense **extent of** country, **no** effort could concentrate
them ; and living wholly by the chase they will probably

---

* Report of Commissioner of **Indian Affairs for 1846–47**: Ex. Docs.,
2nd Sess., 29th Cong., I, 244.

† **The** treaty of 1815 with the Tetons and those of 1815 and 1837 with
the **Yanktons** were made by representatives of only a small portion of
these **large tribes.**

‡ Mdewakantonwan, Wahpekute, Sisseton, and Wahpeton bands.

follow the buffalo and other game as it gradually disappears towards the Rocky Mountains, either in the direction of the head-waters of the Platte or of the Missouri river or both."*

Here it may be noted how large a part the abundance and scarcity of game played in determining the attitude of the Indians toward the Government and *vice versa*. As long as the tribes found it easy to support themselves by the hunt, so long they felt independent and disinclined to look with favor upon overtures for the cession of lands.† In the preamble of the treaty of 1837 with the Mdewakantonwans, it was alleged that they were influenced to cede this portion of their territory by the fact that it was becoming valueless to them for the purpose of hunting. And there can be no doubt that the cession of 1851 was the more easily obtained from the Mississippi Sioux because they realized that their only hope for future subsistence lay in farming and annuities. The inroads of British half-breeds and the pressure of the white population were bringing about a rapid extinction of game.

It is well to note this point here, because from the year 1851 it will be necessary to treat separately the Sioux of the Mississippi and the wilder Sioux of the plains. The easterly bands had then become absolutely dependent upon the Government, and their future, once for all, lay in its hands; the westerly were still independent, because still in possession of broad hunting grounds and, as yet,

---

* Report of the Commissioner of Indian Affairs for 1848, p. 300.

† This same question of subsistence by the hunt determined in large measure their migrations. See Lewis H. Morgan's Indian Migrations, No. Am., 109: 391.

not demoralized by the pernicious system of annuities. Speaking in a broad way, the fate of the former depended upon the governmental policy ; the conduct of the latter temporarily determined that policy.

This same year, then, may be taken as the turning-point in the history of the Sioux. They rose from unimportance to importance in our national councils. Hitherto they had been too remote from the borders either to affect public policy or to be influenced by it. But during the forties the spread of the white population had been rapid beyond all expectation. It was no longer a question of pushing the frontier-line westward. Settlements leaped the line and projected themselves into the very heart of the Indian country. To save the border tribes from extinction, it seemed necessary to throw open wide tracts of land as outlets for the eager emigrants ; and, in order to protect these emigrants, to adopt a conciliatory attitude toward the Indians. The Sioux, numerically of great strength, warlike in their instincts, and possessing a vast territory, became an important factor in the ever more difficult Indian question.

CHAPTER III.

The lamentable condition of the Mississippi Sioux during the latter part of the forties has been described in the previous chapter. The pressure of the white population and the inroads of the British half-breeds were bringing about the rapid extinction of game ; and the Indians were unsuccessful in the small amount of farming which they had attempted. Starvation stared them in the face. On the other hand, it became impossible, indeed it had always been impossible, to enforce the intercourse laws, and emigrants were steadily encroaching upon Indian lands. It was imperative that something be done ; and in July and August of 1851 councils were held with the Mississippi Sioux for the cession of a part of their territory. Two treaties were made with them : one with the Sisseton and Wahpeton, the other with the Mdewakantonwan and Wahpekute bands. By these treaties they ceded all their lands within the boundaries of the present States of Iowa and Minnesota, except a comparatively small district on both sides of the Minnesota river.* The Senate struck out the latter provision and added a supplemental article by which the United States agreed to pay the said tribes ten cents per acre for

---

* " All that tract of country on either side of the Minnesota river from the western boundary of the lands herein ceded, east to the Tchay-tam-bay river on the north, and to the Yellow Medicine river on the south side, to extend, on each side, a distance not less than ten miles from the general course of said river."   U. S. Statutes at Large, X, 949.

the land in the **designated** reservation, and also authorized the President, in the words of the treaty, to "set
apart * * * **such** tracts of country without **the** limits of **the cession** * * * **as** may be satisfactory for
their **future** occupancy **and home** : **provided**, that the
President may, by the consent of these Indians, vary the
conditions aforesaid if deemed expedient."[*]

The United States promised to pay the Sisseton and
Wahpeton bands $1,665,000, as follows : $275,000 to be
paid to the chiefs for the subsistence of the tribes during
the first year after their removal ; $30,000 " to be laid
out under the direction of the President for the establishment of manual-labor schools, the erection of mills and
blacksmiths' shops, opening of farms, fencing and breaking land, and for * * * other beneficial objects * *
* conducive to the prosperity and happiness of said Indians ;" the remainder, $1,360,000, to be held in trust by
the United States and to draw an annual interest of five
per cent. for fifty **years**. This interest was to be applied
thus : $12,000 to be set apart as a " general agricultural
improvement and civilization **fund** ;" $6,000 to be used
for **educational** purposes ; $10,000 to be spent in the
purchase of goods and **provisions** ; and $40,000 to be paid
as a money **annuity.**[†]

The Mdewakantonwan and Wahpekute bands **received**
$1,410,000, to be applied in substantially the **same way.**[‡]

---

[*] U. S. Statutes at Large, X, 952.

[†] *Ibid.*, 949–950.

[‡] $220,000 to be paid to the chiefs for the subsistence of the tribe
one year **after** removal ; $30,000 to be spent for manual-labor schools,
etc.; $1,160,000 to be set apart as a trust fund, and to draw an annual
interest of **five per cent.** for fifty years, interest to be applied as follows :
$12,000 to **be set apart as** a civilization fund ; $6,000 to be used for educational **purposes** ; $10,000 to be spent for goods and provisions; $30,000
to be paid as a money **annuity.** U. S. Statutes at **Large, X,** 954–59.

Before the treaties had been ratified the whites who had been hovering on the borders poured into the country, thus demonstrating once more the inefficiency of the intercourse laws. The Indians were obliged to remain on the ceded lands, for the President had not yet assigned them a reservation. Inevitable confusion resulted, and for the sake of both whites and Indians it became necessary to move the latter. The President then assigned to them for five years the reservation which was to have been theirs by the treaty of 1851. But the Indians were much dissatisfied and little inclined to settle down to agriculture. They felt that it would be a waste of money to improve land which was to be theirs only a short time. They begged that the reservation be secured to them as a permanent home, and this was finally done in 1854.*

The treatment of the Sioux during these years is a striking instance of the short-sighted, wavering, and inconsistent policy of the Government. The Sioux were to devote themselves to agriculture, but they were induced to cede that part of their territory best suited to this purpose, and after much delay settled upon a comparatively poor reservation. They needed instruction in the art of agriculture ; they needed tools and cattle ; but provision was made to apply hardly more than one-half

---

* The act of July 31, 1854, authorized the President "to confirm to the Sioux of Minnesota forever the reserve on the Minnesota river now occupied by them, upon such conditions as he may deem just." U. S. Statutes at Large, X, 326. This confirmation was never formally made. U. S. Statutes at Large, XII, 1038. But the Indians were assured that they might consider the reserve their permanent home. Report of the Commissioner of Indian Affairs for 1854-5 : Sen. Docs., 33d Cong., 2nd Sess., 272.

of their interest annuity to these ends, and the money so applied was neither promptly nor entirely nor carefully spent. The annuities were allowed to fall into arrears, and especially those portions upon whose wise expenditure the progress of the Indians in agriculture depended. Few farmers were provided, and these were seldom competent ; while the tools were often of the poorest grade or inappropriate.* Thus the introduction of the Sioux to their new life was not propitious. They made little progress and felt keenly the difference between their former freedom and their present dependence. This was the condition of affairs at the time of the Spirit Lake massacres. And it was the well-known discontent of the Sioux which led many to believe that they, as a nation, were concerned in this most unfortunate occurrence.

In the early forties the Wahpekute band was under the leadership of two chiefs, one of them, Wamdisapa by name, of notoriously ill-repute. Peace had been made between the Sac and Fox tribe and the Sioux ; but Wamdisapa and his followers still continued hostile, and, moving westward, were gradually separated from the rest of the Wahpekute band. When the treaty of 1851 was made, by which the Sioux of the Mississippi ceded a large

---

* " Have the officers under the President applied those funds so appropriated in the manner stipulated by the treaties ? I can distinctly say, no ! The treaties say these funds shall be annually expended, whereas large amounts have been kept back, and are now in arrear, and after repeated applications to have them expended. These arrears are not mere petty sums, surplusses or remnants of funds remaining unexpended, but large amounts, thousands and tens of thousands, and in some cases the whole fund appropriated for a special purpose." Report of P. Prescott, Superintendent farming for Sioux : Report of Commissioner of Indian Affairs for 1856-7, p. 606 : Ex. Docs., 34th Cong., 3d Sess., Vol. I, Pt. I.

territory, this remnant of Wamdisapa's band was not recognized as a part of the Wahpekute Sioux and took no
part in the treaty. Later, when the annuities were being
paid, some of these Indians appeared at the agency and
insisted upon a share. By 1857 the band, now under
Inkpaduta, consisted of only about half a dozen lodges,
but still retained its lawless and predatory habits. It was
this straggling band that committed the massacres of
Spirit Lake and Springfield in March, 1857, killing
about forty-two persons. As soon as the news reached
the agency efforts were made to overtake and punish the
murderers, but these efforts were unsuccessful. The Mississippi Sioux were then called together and told that
their annuities should cease until the murderers, their
relatives, should have been brought to justice ; and were
required to send out a party in search of them. This the
Sioux at first declined to do unless accompanied by
United States troops. They yielded the point, however,
and sent out an expedition to seek the murderers. But
by this time Inkpaduta's band had divided and the Sioux
party overtook only a portion of it, killing three warriors
and mortally wounding one. Feeling that they had done
their duty they returned home, and the Government re-
sumed the payment of annuities.*

There was a general feeling throughout the country at
this time that we were on the brink of a Sioux war. It
is true that on one occasion a hostile demonstration was
made by the Indians.† But the assertion that the

---

* For a short, clear account of the Inkpaduta War, see Minn. Hist.
Colls., III, 386 ff. See also Report of the Commissioner of Indian Affairs
for 1857-8, pp. 357-9 : Ex. Docs., 35th Cong., 1st Sess., Vol. II, Pt. I.

† See Report of Commissioner of Indian Affairs for 1857-8, p. 388-9 :
Ex. Docs., 35th Cong., 1st Sess., Vol. II, Pt. I.

Mississippi Sioux as a nation were in sympathy with Inkpaduta is utterly without foundation.* The tribal bonds
of these people were very weak and their kinship with
Inkpaduta was a matter of no importance to them. But,
aside from its intrinsic character, the massacre was unfortunate as adding another element to the already dis-
turbed condition of these Sioux.

By the act of July 31, 1854,† the President had been
authorized to confirm to the Minnesota Sioux the reservation upon which they were then situated. This confirmation was never formally made, but was practically
taken for granted in the treaties of 1858.‡ There were
two of these : one with the Lower, the other with the
Upper Sioux ;§ and both provided for the reduction of
this reservation and the assignment of land in severalty.
More specifically, as by treaty with the Upper Sioux July
19, 1858, the terms were these :

Article I provided that so much of the reserve upon
which the Indians were then situated as lay south of the
Minnesota river should constitute a reservation for the
said bands ; should be surveyed and allotted in severalty,
eighty acres to each head of a family or single person
over the age of twenty-one years ; the residue should be
held by the bands in common ; each minor, however,

---

* The most that can be said is that a few of the younger braves and
those influenced by the Yanktons, who felt that their land rights had
been overlooked in the treaties of 1851, sympathized with Inkpaduta.
Ibid., 359.

† U. S. Statutes at Large, X, 326.

‡ *Ibid.*, XII, 1038.

§ The Lower Sioux comprised the Mdewakantonwan and Wahpekute, the Upper Sioux the Sisseton and Wahpeton bands.

upon attaining majority should be given eighty acres
thereof. This same article authorized the President at
his discretion to issue patents for these allotments and to
exempt them "from levy, taxation, sale, or forfeiture
until otherwise provided for by the Legislature of the
State in which they" were "situated, with the assent of
Congress."

Article II provided that, if the Senate agreed, a specific
sum should be allowed these Indians for the land north
of the Minnesota river ; or this land should be sold for
their benefit, they to receive the proceeds of the sale.*

Article VIII provided that such members of the Sisseton and Wahpeton bands as should desire to break their
tribal connections and locate outside of the reservation
should be allowed to do so, and should "be vested with
all the rights, privileges, and immunities, and be subject
to all the laws, obligations, and duties, of the citizens of
the United States."†

---

* "The United States subsequently, by resolution, fixed the price at
thirty cents per acre. This yielded to the lower bands about $96,000,
and to the upper about $240,000." Report of Commissioner of Indian
Affairs for 1863-4, p. 400 : Report of the Sec. of the In., 38th Cong., 1st
Sess., Vol. III.

† There were six other articles. Article III provided that if the
Indians received payment for the lands north of the Minnesota river
such a sum as should be found necessary, not, however, to exceed
$70,000, should be set aside to pay their just debts and to provide goods
for them.

Article IV provided that all Indian intercourse laws be in force over
the land retained under Article I.

Article V gave the United States the right to maintain military posts
and construct roads on the reservation, due compensation being made.

Article VI provided for the preservation of peace between the
United States and the said bands.

These treaties are good exponents of the national policy of these years. The reservation of the Sioux was no larger than the needs of an agricultural life justified ; provision was made for the allotment of land in severalty ; the Secretary of the Interior was given "discretionary power in regard to the manner and objects of the annual expenditure" of the money due the bands by former treaties and to become due by this.

The immediate causes of these treaties were two. First, the white population of Minnesota was increasing so rapidly that already the need of more land was felt. Second, there was a real desire on the part of the Government to advance the welfare of these bands who seemed now ready for an agricultural life. Of these two causes, it cannot be denied that the first was of paramount importance. To this conclusion we are forced by the fact that the Government's interest in the welfare of these Indians was not strong enough to impel it to fulfill its obligations toward them. The old trouble continued. The annuities were in arrears. The goods sent were of inferior quality and not of the kind most needed. Despite these drawbacks, however, the Indians progressed, and by 1860 it was possible to divide them into two classes—farmer and blanket Indians. The farmer Indians were

---

Article VII provided for the withholding of annuities from intoxicated Indians.

Article IX gave the Secretary of the Interior discretion "over the manner and objects of the annual expenditure."

U. S. Statutes at Large, XII, 1037-41.

The treaty with the Lower Sioux, made June 19, 1858, did not contain Article VIII. See U. S. Statutes at Large, edited by G. P. Sanger, 36th Cong., 79-84. This is the only reference I have made to this edition of the Statutes.

those who were devoting themselves to agriculture
and were adopting, to some extent, the habits and customs of a white community ; the blanket Indians, those
who still clung to the old savage life. It lay in the
nature of the case that these two classes should be
strongly antagonistic. It was a struggle between barbarism and civilization. The policy of the Government
aimed at civilization, and, as far as it went, was well suited
to that end. Land in severalty and education were to
bring home to the Sioux a sense of individual responsibility. But no provision was made for the protection of
the civilized from the blanket Indian. The latter was
left even freer than he had been before, for the power of
the chief over him was weakened and its place supplied
by no other restraint. Except for inefficient intercourse
laws, the Government thus left uncontrolled an element
whose pleasure it would be to strike a blow at civilization
at the first opportunity.

There were still other unfortunate circumstances. Almost from the first there had been a continual wrangling
over the treaties of 1858. While they were being drawn
up, the Sioux had been led to expect that they would
receive a certain sum of money in cash. In this they
were misinformed, for the treaties contained no such provision ; but to them the spoken word was as sacred as the
written. There was another misunderstanding which
concerned the amount to be used in payment for depredations. The Lower Sioux fund and about two-thirds of
Upper Sioux fund were exhausted to pay the debts of the
Indians,* although each of the treaties stipulated that not

---

* Report of the Commissioner of Indian Affairs for 1863-4, p. 400 :
Report of the Sec. of the In., 38th Cong., 1st Sess., Vol. III.

more than seventy thousand dollars should be used for this purpose. Add to this the fact that the annuities were not promptly paid,* and we can readily understand that the Sioux felt themselves ill-treated. Moreover, the Civil War was going on, and the Indians were made restless and uneasy by all sorts of exaggerated stories of the pending fall of the Government. Their faith in the strength and dignity of their "Great Father" received a shock, and they felt that their support rested upon an unstable basis. There can be little doubt that stray secessionists fostered this feeling; and the British half-breeds of the North not only sympathized with the Indians but stood ready to furnish them with guns, powder, and ammunition.

The spark which lighted this inflammable material was the murder of six whites, committed by fourteen intoxicated Lower Sioux, August 17, 1862. Feeling that unless there was a general uprising they would be pursued and individually punished, the murderers hastened to their kinsmen and urged them to take up arms. By the next morning they had increased their party to two hundred, and now proceeded to the Lower Agency, sending runners ahead with the message that all who did not join them should be punished with death. Many of the farmer Indians were thus practically forced to take part. Little Crow became leader and the work of devastation began. It is estimated that nearly one thousand whites lost their lives in the massacres which now took place.

---

* The financial straits occasioned by the Civil War may serve, at least in part, to exonerate the Government from blame. The delay was only four or five weeks, and there was no fixed time for the payment of the Sioux annuities. They had, however, been paid in July, the year before, and the Indians naturally expected them in the same month.

Major General Sibley was dispatched to quell the outbreak, and about seventeen hundred persons either surrendered to him or were captured by him. A large number of the warriors were tried by a military commission
and sentenced to death. Of these thirty-nine were hanged,
an attempt having been made to select those who had
personally committed acts of violence. The remainder of
those who had surrendered, together with some of the peace-
ably disposed Sioux, were removed to Crow Creek, May,
1863.* A small number of those who had continued
faithful to the Government remained in Minnesota.
About two hundred of the Sioux were held as prisoners
of war at Davenport. About six or eight hundred, who
claimed that they had taken no part in the massacres but
had fled from Minnesota to avoid the indiscriminate
vengeance of the whites, were in the vicinity of Fort
Wadsworth, Dakota. The remainder, made up largely
of the really hostile Indians and those who had committed crimes and feared the punishment of the Government, had taken refuge far to the north in or near the
British Possessions. These, together with some of the
Missouri Sioux who had joined them for reasons that
will be stated in the next chapter, continued hostile for
many years, and, though not actively engaged in warfare
during the whole time, were not subdued until the
seventies.

The selection of the Crow Creek reservation proved
most unfortunate. It was not adapted to the purpose of

---

* These Sioux were nearly all women and children, there being only
about one hundred able-bodied men. The Crow Creek reservation was
selected under authority of the act of March 3, 1863: U. S. Statutes at
Large, XII, 819-20.

agriculture, and for three successive years the crops failed. In 1866 these Indians were moved to Niobrara, where they were joined by those who had been held as prisoners at Davenport. In the fall of the same year they were moved to the mouth of Bazile creek, and in 1868 to Breckinridge, ten miles below the mouth of the Niobrara.*

The condition of the Indians during these years was very wretched. The act of February 16, 1863,† had annulled all treaties previously made with them so far as these treaties purported "to impose any future obligation on the United States." The annuities and claims of the Mississippi Sioux were thus declared forfeited. The act of March 3, 1863,‡ had authorized the President to set apart for them "a tract of unoccupied land outside of the limits of any State, sufficient in extent to enable him to assign to each member * * * eighty acres of good agricultural lands." But five years elapsed before the Indians were settled upon a reservation, and during this period they were moved four times. All of these removals were attended with the greatest hardships and sufferings.§

Meanwhile these Indians, from this time on generally

---

* This reserve had been set apart for their use by President Johnson under the Executive Orders of February 27, 1866, and November 16, 1867: Report of the Commissioner of Indian Affairs for 1886, p. 340.

† U. S. Statutes at Large, XII, 652.

‡ *Ibid.*, 819. This same act provided for the sale of the Minnesota reservation and the expenditure of the proceeds for the benefit of the Indians in their new homes; but such sale could not take place immediately.

§ For a description of the terrible suffering attending these removals, see Manypenny, Our Indian Wards, 135 ff. The picture may be somewhat overdrawn, but it is substantially true.

called the Santee Sioux, were wholly dependent upon the bounty of the Government. The fact that they had no treaty relations with the United States made them feel insecure, and they begged that an agreement of some kind be made with them. This was done April 29, 1868.[*] The treaty provided for the allotment of land in severalty, for the compulsory education of all children between the ages of six and sixteen, and the employment of a teacher for every thirty of such children, and for the distribution of certain goods.[†]

Allotments were now made these Indians both under the act of March 3, 1863, and the treaty of April 29, 1868. Patents were not issued for the allotments and the allottees did not become citizens of the United States. Later, by the act making appropriations for the fiscal year ending June 30, 1884,[‡] the patents to the land allotted under the treaty of 1868 were declared of legal effect ; and the United States promised to hold the land in trust for twenty-five years, and at the end of that time to deliver it to the Indians or their heirs "free of all charge or incumbrance."

By the act of February 9, 1885,[§] the Santee reservation was thrown open to settlement.

By Section 7 of the act of March 2, 1889,[||] all allotments made to the Santee Sioux in Nebraska were con-

---

* U. S. Statutes at Large, XV, 635–640.

† The provisions of this treaty are given at length in connection with the Sioux of the Plains. See Chapter IV.

‡ U. S. Statutes at Large, XXII, 433.

§ Report of Commissioner of Indian Affairs for 1886, p. 342.

|| Report of Commissioner of Indian Affairs for 1889, p. 450.

firmed ; and it was provided that those who had not received allotments should be given them upon the reserve in Nebraska as follows : "To each head of a family, one-quarter of a section ; to each single person over eighteen years of age, one-eighth of a section ; to each orphan child under eighteen years of age, one-eighth of a section ; to each other person under eighteen years of age now living, one-sixteenth of a section."

Thus all the Santee Sioux on the reserve in Nebraska were provided with land.

A word now about a portion of these Sioux not located on the reserve. Between 1868 and 1875 about eighty-five families took up homesteads under the concluding paragraph of Article VI of the treaty of 1868,* forty-six miles north of Sioux Falls, Dakota, on the Big Sioux river. They, of course, became citizens of the United States and were subject to and protected by the laws of the United States. But on taking lands the Indians were obliged to renounce all claims for annuities.† They had

---

* This provided that any male over eighteen years of age, party to this treaty, who should settle upon land outside of the reservation and open to Indian occupation, occupy the same for three successive years and make improvements thereon to the value of two hundred dollars, should receive a patent for one hundred and sixty acres and become a citizen of the United States.

† It has been suggested that this unjust requirement of the Indian Department was based on the refusal of the House to sanction the treaty of 1868. I quote Mr. Paine's words to the House : "Let us never again recognize any constitutional right on the part of the President of the United States, by and with the advice and consent of the Senate, to negotiate a treaty with an Indian tribe, as a sovereign power, as a foreign nation. If it be a contract of valid moral obligation, let us fulfill it ; but let us never again, by any legislation to which this House shall give its consent, sanctify it as a treaty between sovereign powers.

"Now, if these Indians referred to in the Senate amendment have

a hard time of it for three or four years. Then the Government came to their aid and generously assisted them. They received also their just share of the proceeds from the sale of the Minnesota reservation.

All of the Santee Sioux made great progress. They applied themselves to agriculture and succeeded well. For a time the United States assisted them with liberal appropriations, but these were gradually diminished as the Indians became self-supporting. At present only the aged and infirm receive rations. The Indian question, so far as the Santee Sioux are concerned, has been settled.

After the massacres of 1862, six or eight hundred Sisseton and Wahpeton Sioux had fled to avoid quick vengeance at the hands of the whites. Many were really innocent and had voluntarily surrendered to General Sibley. These were located near Fort Wadsworth. Others of the Sisseton and Wahpeton Sioux had remained in the vicinity of their Minnesota reservation, preserving their treaty relations with the United States, and doing much to protect the whites from the hostile bands. With these two classes the Government made a treaty February 19, 1867.* The chief provisions of this treaty, as amended by the Senate, were as follows :

Article II gave "the United States the right to construct wagon-roads, railroads, mail stations, telegraph

---

any just claim against the Government of the United States, let us pay it fully; but let us not consent to this Senate amendment, which requires us to make this appropriation because in 1867 and in 1869 the President and the Senate agreed by treaty to do it." Congressional Globe, 41st Cong., 2d Sess., Pt. 6, p. 5008.

* U. S. Statutes at Large, XV, 505–11; Ratification advised with amendments April 15, 1867; Amendments accepted April 22, 1867.

lines, and * * * other public improvements " over
the lands claimed by these Indians,* including their
reservation, as afterwards designated.

Article III provided that a certain tract of land in the
central eastern part of Dakota† be set aside for those
members of the bands who had surrendered to the Government and had not been sent to Crow Creek, and for
those who had been released from prison in 1866.

Article IV provided that a certain tract of land in the
northern part of Dakota‡ be set apart for all other members of the said bands who had not been sent to Crow
Creek, and also for the Cuthead band of Yanktonnais
Sioux.

Article V provided that the two reservations " be ap-
portioned in tracts of (160) one hundred and sixty acres
to each head of a family, or single person over the age of
(21) twenty-one years " ; and that every person who

---

* " Said lands so claimed being bounded on the south and east by
the treaty line of 1851 and the Red river of the North to the mouth of
Goose river, on the north by the Goose river and a line running from
the source thereof by the most easterly point of Devil's lake to the
Chief's Bluff at the head of James river, and on the west by the James
river, and thence to Kampeska lake." U. S. Statutes at Large, XV, 506.

† " Beginning at the head of Lake Traverse [E], and thence along
the treaty line of the treaty of 1851 to Kampeska lake ; thence in a
direct line to Reipan or the northeast point of the Cateare des Prairie
[S], and thence passing north of Skunk lake, on the most direct line of
1851 to the place of beginning." *Ibid.* See second map.

‡ " Beginning at the most easterly point of Devil's lake; thence
along the waters of said lake to the most westerly point of the same ;
thence on a direct line to the nearest point on the Cheyenne river ;
thence down said river to a point opposite the lower end of Aspen island,
and thence on a direct line to the place of beginning." U. S. Statutes
at Large, XV, 506. See second map.

should receive an allotment and should "occupy and
cultivate a portion thereof for five consecutive years *
* * be entitled to receive a patent for the same " so
soon as he should have fifty acres " fenced, ploughed,
and in crop " : provided that such a patent should not
authorize any transfer of any portion of the land except
to the United States ; but the lands should " descend to
the proper heirs of the person obtaining a patent."*

Article VI provided that Congress should, " at its own
discretion, from time to time, make such appropriations "
as should be deemed " requisite to enable said Indians
to return to an agricultural life."†

Article VII provided that an agent be immediately
located at Lake Traverse and one at Devil's lake so soon
as five hundred persons be settled there.

Article VIII provided that " no goods, provisions,
groceries, or other articles—except materials for the
erection of houses and articles to facilitate the operations
of agriculture— * * * be issued * * * unless it
be in payment of labor performed, or for produce delivered."‡

Article IX provided that " no person be authorized to
trade for furs or peltries within the limits of the land
claimed by said bands * * * and that no person,
not a member of said bands, * * * except persons
in the employ of the Government, or located under its
authority, * * * be permitted to locate upon said

---

* U. S. Statutes at Large, XV, 506.

† *Ibid.*, 507.

‡ *Ibid.*

lands either for hunting, trapping, or agricultural purposes."*

In accordance with the provisions of this treaty these
Indians were located on two reservations : one at Devil's
lake, covering approximately two hundred and seventy-
five thousand acres of good prairie land, the other at
Lake Traverse and containing about nine hundred and
eighteen thousand seven hundred and eighty acres of
equally good land.   Here they began once more an agricultural life and became the best exponents of the governmental policy of the ensuing years.   Land was allotted
them in severalty and annuities paid, as a rule, only for
work done.   The Indians progressed rapidly ; and there
can be no doubt that this was largely due to the earnest
efforts of the American Board and the Presbyterian
Board of Missions.   This feature of President Grant's
peace policy worked admirably here.

September 20, 1872, an agreement was made with the
Lake Traverse and Devil's Lake Indians, by which they
ceded any right which they might possess to the land
referred to in the second article of the treaty of 1867.
This agreement, as amended by the Senate and ratified†

---

* U. S. Statutes at Large, XV, 507.

There were two other articles.

Article I provided for the continuation of friendly relations between
the United States and the said bands.

Article X authorized the chiefs and head men to adopt such rules as
seemed best to them " for the security of life and property, the advancement of civilization and the agricultural prosperity of the members of
said bands, and to organize a force for the carrying out of the same and
of such regulations as might be prescribed by the Interior Department."
U. S. Statutes at Large, XV, 507.

† May 19, 1873.

by the Sioux, was confirmed in the Indian Appropriation
Act of June 22, 1874.* In consideration of their cession
the bands received eight hundred thousand dollars, to be
paid in ten annual installments, and " to be expended,
under the direction of the President of the United States,
on the plan and in accordance with the provisions of the
treaty, dated February 19, 1867, for goods and provisions ; for the erection of manual-labor and public
schoolhouses, and for the support of manual-labor and
public schools ; and in the erection of mills, blacksmiths' shops, and other workshops * * * and such
other beneficial objects as may be deemed most conducive to the prosperity and happiness of the Sisseton and
Wahpeton bands."†

Nearly seventeen years elapsed before the Sioux
entered into the next agreement with the United
States. This time it was for the reduction of their reservation as provided in the fifth section of the Land in
Severalty Bill. All the Indians on the Lake Traverse
reservation having received allotments, it was thought
best to throw open the unallotted lands to white settlers.
Accordingly an agreement was made with these Sioux
December 12, 1889, which was ratified March 3, 1891.‡
This agreement provided that there should be allotted to
each individual member of the bands such a quantity
of land as would make, together with that already

---

* For the agreement as originally made, see Report of the Commissioner of Indian Affairs for 1872, 122-3. The Senate amended this by
striking out the paragraphs numbered, respectively, third, fourth, fifth,
sixth, seventh, eighth, and ninth.

† Report of the Commissioner of Indian Affairs for 1872, p. 122.

‡ U. S. Statutes at Large, XXVI, 1035-8.

allotted, one hundred and sixty acres ; and, in case no allotment had been made to any individual, then such an one should receive an allotment of one hundred and sixty acres.   The object of this provision was to equalize the allotments so that each member of the bands, including married women, might have the same amount of land.*   All were to have patents issued to them upon the " terms and conditions " of the Land in Severalty Bill.

The Indians ceded the land, which should be left when the above provision should be carried into effect, to the United States for two dollars and fifty cents an acre.   This money was to be held in the Treasury of the United States for the sole use of the Sioux, was to draw three per cent. interest, and was " to be at all times subject to appropriation by Congress for the education and civilization of the said bands."†

The third article of this agreement provided that the sum of $342,778.37 be paid the Indians, as " being the amount * * * due certain members * * * who served in the armies of the United States against their own people " in the war of 1862, " and of which they had been wrongfully and unjustly deprived " by the act of February 16, 1863.‡   It was further agreed to pay

---

* This was also the object of the act of February 28, 1891, which amended the General Allotment Act so as to provide for the same allotment of land to each member of the tribe, regardless of his age or status.

† U. S. Statutes at Large, XXVI, 1036.

‡ See U. S. Statutes at Large, XII, 652.   This act annulled the treaties made with these bands and thus deprived them of their annuities.   The sum of $342,778.37 granted these Indians was "at the rate of $18,400 per annum from July 1, 1862, to July 1, 1888, less their pro rata share of the sum of $616,086.52 heretofore appropriated for the benefit of said Sisseton and Wahpeton bands."

them the sum of $18,400 annually from July 1, 1888, to
July 1, 1901, the latter being the date at which the annuities of the treaty of 1851 were to cease.

It has been said that since this reservation was
thrown open to white settlers the Indians have deterio-
rated. But the time has been too brief to justify such a
positive statement. It may be that the necessity of ad-
justing themselves to a new environment has temporarily retarded their progress. But it was an adjustment
which had to take place sooner or later, and, once made,
progress will begin again, and will continue more steadily and rapidly than before.

Allotment at Devil's lake was slower than at Lake
Traverse, but in 1893 nearly all the Indians were living
upon and cultivating land in severalty ; the residue was
held in common. The Devil's Lake Indians had had
some trouble about their boundary line as established by
the fourth article of the treaty of February 19, 1867. The
line was run in 1875, and its correctness was not questioned until 1883, when it was discovered that it deprived
them of about sixty-four thousand acres of land which
was lawfully theirs. By this time a large number of
whites, believing the land a part of the public domain,
had settled upon it. It was plain that these could not be
removed, but it was equally plain that the Indians ought
to be compensated. No action was taken, however, until
June 30, 1892, when Congress enacted that these bands
be paid for the sixty-four thousand acres at the rate of
one dollar and twenty-five cents per acre ; "this amount
to be expended under the direction of the Secretary of
the Interior in the purchase of stock and agricultural implements, and in promoting the comfort and improve-

ment of said Indians,"* eighty thousand dollars to be immediately available.

The last reports† of the Devil's Lake Indians have not been so encouraging as those of former years. The relapse, however, may have been only temporary. This certainly is to be hoped, for these Indians will soon have to look to themselves for support. Except for the unallotted lands on their reservation, they have nothing from which they can obtain any revenue, and they cannot depend upon the bounty of the Government. But, if we may judge the future by the past, the outlook is hopeful rather than otherwise. During the seventies and eighties these Indians made comparatively rapid progress, evincing considerable capacity in taking on the habits and customs of civilized man. The testimony of these years must incline us to hope that ultimately the Devil's Lake Indians will take their place as intelligent and self-supporting Indians.

---

* U. S. Statutes at Large, XXVI, 1010.

† See Report of the Commissioner of Indian Affairs for 1893, pp. 228–30; *ibid.* for 1894, pp. 216–18.

CHAPTER IV.

THE SIOUX OF THE PLAINS FROM 1850 TO 1893.

In 1850 the Sioux of the Plains comprised that part of the great Sioux family roaming over the country of the Missouri and Upper Platte rivers. They were a wild but brave people, wholly dependent upon the chase for subsistence, and as yet not bound to the United States by treaty relations. It was, of course, impossible to obtain an accurate knowledge of their number, but the Commissioner of Indian Affairs for 1853–4 estimated it to be nearly sixteen thousand—the Brulé band containing about one hundred and fifty lodges, the Yankton three hundred and seventy-five, the Yanktonnais four hundred and fifty, the Blackfeet one hundred and fifty, the Uncpapa two hundred and eighty, the Sans Arc one hundred and sixty, and the Minneconjou two hundred and twenty-five.*

Previous to 1850 these Sioux had had little intercourse with the whites. Living remote from our frontiers, their wild mode of life had been uninterrupted and uninfluenced by civilization. But the rapid territorial growth of the United States between 1840 and 1850 and the consequent immigration changed their status, together with that of the other wilder tribes.

The causes which stimulated western immigration have already been discussed in Chapter I. Right of transit

---

* For the general location of these bands, see Report of Commissioner of Indian Affairs for 1853–4, p. 353 : Sen. Doc., 33d Cong., 1st Sess., I.

through the Indian country was absolutely necessary to the immigrants, whose number had increased one hundred-fold since the discovery of gold in California in 1848 ; and February 17, 1851, a treaty was made at Fort Laramie with eight tribes, of which the Sioux were one.* The United States obtained from these Indians permission to establish roads and military posts on their territory, and in return promised to protect them from the depredations of the whites, and to pay them in goods annually for fifty years the sum of fifty thousand dollars, to be distributed among them in proportion to their population. In this same treaty boundaries between the various tribes were established, and the Indians promised to refrain from hostilities against each other. The Senate amended the treaty, limiting the annuity to ten years and giving the President discretionary power to continue it five years longer. This amendment was subsequently ratified by all† save the Crows. But since the United States was dealing with the tribes jointly and not severally, the failure of the Crows to sign made the ratification invalid and the amended treaty of no effect.‡ Despite this fact, the Government ordered the annuities to be stopped promptly at the end of fifteen years, and this was one of the main causes of the war of 1866.

---

* The other tribes were the Cheyenne, Arapahoe, Crow, Assinaboin, Gros Ventre, Mandan, and Arickaree.

† Only four of the six Sioux chiefs who signed the treaty signed the amendment. Possibly this would have impaired its validity for them, even supposing it had been valid in all other respects.

‡ For this reason the treaty is not to be found in any of our public statutes. I was able to obtain a copy of it only through the Secretary of State.

Considering the fact that these Indians were dependent upon the chase for subsistence, and that game rapidly decreased in consequence of the steady stream of immigration, the annuity was miserably small. Many of the Sioux eked out a living with roots, herbs, and berries ; some really suffered from starvation. In addition to this, the Indians were stricken with smallpox, measles, and cholera, diseases which they claimed, and with some reason, had been introduced among them by the immigrants.

Despite their sad plight, the Sioux essentially kept the treaty of 1851, until the annihilation of Lieutenant Grattan's command in 1854 ; and the circumstances which led to this unfortunate affair were such as to exonerate them from blame. On August 18 of that year a company of Mormon emigrants passed an encampment of Brulé, Ogallala, and Minneconjou Indians waiting near Fort Laramie for their annuities. A cow belonging to one of the emigrants strayed into the Indian village and was there killed by a Minneconjou, who then took refuge with the Brulés. The Bear, chief of the Brulés, went to Fort Laramie, reported the circumstances and advised that troops be sent to demand the culprit. Accordingly, the next day, August 19, Lieutenant Grattan, with a party of twenty-nine men, went to the Indian camp. But the Bear either could not or would not deliver up the offender. Several circumstances unite to give weight to the former supposition. First, it is not probable that the Bear would have gone to Fort Laramie and advised that a detachment of troops be sent to demand the offender, if he had not intended to use such power as he had to influence his camp to deliver up the

Indian. Second, the chiefs of these western tribes had very little authority, and that which the Bear had was counteracted by the conduct of Lieutenant Grattan's drunken interpreter, whose brutal language incensed the Indians. However that may be, the culprit was not delivered up, and Lieutenant Grattan and his party, armed and taking with them a twelve-pounder and a mountain howitzer, made their way into the village and attempted to take him by force. There they were surrounded and killed to a man.* Immediately afterwards the Indians went to the warehouse near by and took from it their annuity goods.†

The Sioux tribes did not regard this massacre as a signal for a general uprising. As a whole they remained quiet and peaceable as before. But a few bands, led by the wilder and younger braves, committed some depredations and made raids upon neighboring tribes ; and one of them, Wasagahas' band, murdered a United States mail party in November, 1854. These troubles were greatly exaggerated, and General Harney with three regiments was dispatched to put an end to the " Sioux War." The North Platte was declared the boundary be-

---

* The above account has been taken from the Reports of the Commissioner of Indian Affairs and Reports from the Department of the West: Ex. Docs , 33rd Cong., 2nd Sess., Vol. I, Pt. II, No. I, pp. 38–40.

† The Commissioner of Indians affairs, in commenting upon this unhappy event, says: "The Mormons should, under the provisions of the 'intercourse act,' have applied to the agent, who was in the vicinity, for redress, and he could, under the law, have paid, out of the annuities, for the property taken ; but no officer of the military department was, in my opinion, authorized to arrest or try the Indian for the offense charged against him." Report of the Commissioner of Indian Affairs for 1854-5. Sen. Doc., 33d Cong., 2nd Sess., I, 224.

tween the hostile and friendly Indians, and all, except
those of the Brulé band, who had been implicated in the
United States mail murder and those who had committed
depredations upon the whites were ordered to cross to
the south side of the river. For some reason Little
Thunder and his band of Brulé Sioux* remained on the
north side, encamped on Blue Water creek. Here they
were attacked by General Harney, September 3, 1855.
Eighty-six Indians were killed, five wounded, seventy
women and children captured, fifty mules and ponies
taken, and an indefinite number killed and disabled.
This Battle of the Blue Water was the only one of moment in the so-called Sioux War of 1855.†

The next year, at a council held during the first five days
of March, an attempt was made to adjust the difficulties
between the United States and the Sioux. The records
of this council portray most admirably the temper of the
Indians there represented : " The Two Kettle, Lower
Yanctons, Uncpapas, Blackfeet Sioux, Minneconjous, Sans
Arc, Yanctonnais, two bands, and Brulés of the Platte."‡
The chiefs sincerely deprecated the wrongs which had
been committed by their people, and deeply desired

---

* There seems to be some question as to whether these Indians had
anything to do with the Grattan massacre. General Harney says he
found in their possession remnants of clothing, etc., carried off by
the Indians on that occasion, and that would seem to implicate them.
On the other hand, the agent, Thomas S. Twiss, invited them to cross to
the South Platte, although he had forbidden the Grattan murderers to
do so. See Ex. Docs., 34th Cong., 1st Sess., Vol. I, Pt. II, p. 51; *ibid.*,
Pt. I, 401.

† For an account of the battle in General Harney's own words, see
Ex. Docs., 34th Cong., 1st Sess., Vol. I, Pt. 2, pp. 49–51.

‡ *Ibid.*, Vol. XII, No. 130, p. 6.

peace. The attitude of General Harney was admirable.
Throughout the council he impressed the Indians with
the idea that the United States was all powerful and
would insist upon the strictest adherence to treaty rights ;
and that every infringement of these would be surely
punished. Finally, he submitted to them a treaty which
was signed by the nine bands named above, and later by
the Ogallalas, who had not been represented at this
council. The Indians, on their part, promised to deliver
up to the nearest military post all who had "committed
murders or other outrages upon white persons"* and all
stolen property. The chiefs were to be responsible for
the good conduct of their bands, and, if not able to
control them, were to report the fact to the nearest military post. The Indians were not to molest, but, on the
contrary, to protect travelers through their country.
Sioux war parties were not to go down to the Pawnee
country. Trade in horses and mules was to be stopped
because it encouraged young men to steal. The Indians
were advised " to raise stock and to cultivate the soil."†

The United States, on its part, engaged to protect the
Sioux from impositions by the whites ; to restore the
annuities, and to set at liberty all Indian prisoners "not
implicated in any murder, robbery, or other high crime
against our people." These were the terms of the treaty,
but the Indians laid quite as much stress upon the suggestions and promises of General Harney, which did not
receive treaty sanction. What these were may be most
clearly seen from his own words :

" Certain chiefs were recognized by the nation, others

---

* Ex. Docs., 34th Cong., 1st Sess., Vol. XII, No. 130, p. 6.

† Ex. Docs., 34th Cong., 1st Sess., Vol. XII, No. 130, pp. 6-7.

by the military, others again by the agents, and the
traders, for their own purposes, have most unwarranta-
bly given medals and appointed chiefs. These conflicting interests necessarily weakened the authority of all
these chiefs, and to correct this evil I most respectfully
request that the President will direct and order that
hereafter none other chiefs of the Sioux but those selected in the late council, under the conditions there agreed
upon, be recognized by either the War or Interior De-
partments. This unity of action will greatly tend to
promote the influence of the Government over these
people. That the organization of the Sioux may be more
complete, I proposed to the chiefs to have a certain number of soldiers in each band to assist them to carry out
my views. They have each given in the number which
they deemed sufficient for that purpose in each band,
and I recommend that these soldiers be regularly named,
and receive from the Government a dress or uniform by
which they will be known ; and that for the time they
may be doing duty under their chiefs in their villages
they will receive their rations. The expense would be
trifling, and their young men would be stimulated and
encouraged to seek these positions. The dress should be
durable and gaudy, particularly the head-dress (they are
fond of feathers). The uniform of the different bands
should be different, and the same should have place in
the different grades of chief, sub-chief, etc. By gradually
causing the interests of a portion of the nation to depend
upon the wishes of the Government, the remainder will
be easily controlled."*

* Ex. Docs., 34th Cong., 1st Sess., Vol. XII, No. 130, p. 3.

In his council* with these Indians General Harney recognized certain chiefs as the only head chiefs of their respective bands, and stipulated the number of soldiers each chief was to have. He also forwarded to the President an estimate of the amount necessary to fulfill the agreements made with the Indians, the amount being sixty-two thousand dollars.

Although General Harney was authorized by the President to make the treaty, it does not appear that it was ever looked upon as legal. It was never published in the statutes, and neither party strictly adhered to it. The plan proposed to remedy the inability of the chiefs to restrain their young braves received little encouragement, and soon died a natural death. It is to be regretted that the plan was not carried out, for it struck to the root of the trouble and might have furnished a remedy. As it was, neither the Harney campaign nor the so-called "Harney treaty" met with a definite result.

The next few years were uneventful. There were raids and depredations upon the whites, but none of serious magnitude. With the exception of several small bands of Santees on the Minnesota river who did not receive annuities, there were no actively hostile Sioux. Still, the security for continued peace was not strong. The treaty of Fort Laramie in 1851 had been made by a meagre representation of the tribes, and not all of the Missouri Sioux felt themselves bound by it; and those who did not were the most warlike and independent of their people. They resented the encroachments of the whites upon their territory and desired to have absolute-

---

* For the minutes of this council, see *ibid.*, No. 130.

ly nothing to do with the Government. They insisted, moreover, that those who had signed this treaty should repudiate their obligations and refuse to receive annuities.

On the other hand, those who had signed the Fort Laramie treaty were at the mercy of this hostile element. They repeatedly begged the Government to aid them, but no attention was paid to their request. Still they continued loyal until 1862. When, in May of that year, the agent arrived at Fort Pierre with their annuity goods, they held a consultation and then, once more, explained their position. They said : "That General Harney, at Pierre, in 1856, had promised them aid ; that they were greatly in the minority ; that that portion of their people opposed to the Government were more hostile than ever before ; that they had, year after year, been promised the fulfillment of this pledge, but since none had come they must now break off their friendly relations with the Government and rejoin their respective bands, as they could hold out no longer ; that their lives and property were threatened in case they accepted any more goods from the Government ; that the small amount of annuities given them did not give satisfaction ; it created discord rather than harmony, nor would it justify them to come in so far to receive them ; that they had been friends to the Government and to all white men ; had lived up to their pledges made at Laramie in 1857, as far as it was possible under the circumstances, and still wished to do so, but must henceforth be excused unless their Great Father would aid them."*

* Report of Samuel N. Latta, United States agent, Upper Missouri : Report of Commissioner of Indian Affairs for 1862-3, 37th Cong., 3rd

Meanwhile the travel of the whites through the Indian country westward continued. Many of them committed depredations, and, despite the guarantee* of the United States to the Indians in the treaty of 1851, were left unpunished. It is, therefore, not surprising that the fall of 1862 found many of the Missouri Sioux actively hostile. When they were joined by the Santee† fugitives of Minnesota, the Government had upon its hands a war of no mean proportions. The number of the hostiles rapidly increased. There being no military posts on the Upper Missouri to protect the friendly Indians, they were obliged in self-defense to take up arms. In 1864 war broke out with the Cheyennes and Arapahoes. More United States troops were sent, but the difficulty of "conquering a peace" seemed as great as ever. Finally a Commission‡ was appointed by the President to treat with the bands of the Upper Missouri. The first council was held at Fort Sully, October 6, 1865, with the chiefs

Sess., II, p. 336. **The fear of the Indians was** justified. Bear's Rib, chief of the Uncpapas, was killed by the Sans Arcs for allowing his band to accept annuities. Report of the Commissioner of Indian Affairs for 1862–3: Report of the Secretary of the Interior, 37th Cong., 3d Sess., Vol. II, 184–5.

* The third article of this treaty read as follows : "The **United States** bind themselves to protect the aforesaid Indian nations against **the com**mission of all depredations by the people of the said **United** States, after the ratification of this **treaty.**" Copy of treaty obtained **from** the Secretary of the Interior.

† **Another name for** the Sioux of the Mississippi. From 1860 on they are often **called the Santee** Sioux.

‡ **The members of this** Commission were Newton Edmun, Edward B. Taylor, Major-General S. R. **Curtis,** Brigadier-General H. H. Sibley, Henry W. Reed, and Orrin Guernsey.

and head men of the Minneconjou, and on the tenth a treaty* was made with them.

Article I provided that the Minneconjou acknowledge the jurisdiction and authority of the United States, bind themselves to cease all hostilities against it, and use their influence to prevent other Sioux bands or adjacent tribes from making hostile demonstrations.

Article II provided that the Minneconjou "discontinue for the future all attacks upon the persons or property of other tribes, unless first assailed by them."

Article III provided that " all controversies or differences arising between the Minneconjou band of Dakotas or Sioux, represented in council, and other tribes of Indians, involving the question of peace or war, * * * be submitted to the arbitrament of the President, or * * * persons designated by him, and the decision or award faithfully observed by the said band represented in council."

Article IV provided that the Indians withdraw " from the routes overland already established, or hereafter to be established through their country"; and that the United States pay to them the sum of ten thousand dollars annually for twenty years in such articles as the Secretary of the Interior might direct.

Article V provided that any individual locating permanently on lands belonging to their band be protected therein "against any annoyance or molestation on the part of whites or Indians."

Article VI provided that any amendment made by the

---

* U. S. Statutes at Large, XIV, 695-6.

Senate be binding upon the band without its ratification.*

Treaties embracing the same articles, but differing in
the amount of the annuity promised each band,† were
made during the same month of October with the Blackfeet,‡ the Lower Brulé, the Ogallala, the Uncpapa, the
Sans Arc, the Two Kettle, the Yanktonnais, and the
Upper Yanktonnais Sioux.§ Those with the last six
bands embraced an additional article which provided, in
the words of the treaty, " that whenever twenty lodges or
families of the —— band shall have located on land for
agricultural purposes, * * * they, as well as other
families so locating, shall receive the sum of twenty-five
dollars annually, for five years, for each family, in agricultural implements and improvements ; and when one

---

* This is interesting as showing how completely the theory and
practice of the United States were at variance. These Indians were
theoretically regarded as nations, but a treaty with a nation would not
have contained such an article as this.

† The Blackfeet were promised $7,000 annually for twenty years.
The Lower Brulés were promised $6,000 annually for twenty years.
The Ogallalas were promised $10,000 annually for twenty years.
The Uncpapas were promised $30 for each family annually for
twenty years.
The Sans Arcs were promised $30 for each family annually for
twenty years.
The Two Kettles were promised $6,000 annually for twenty years.
The Yanktonnais were promised $30 for each family annually for
twenty years.
The Upper Yanktonnais were promised $10,000 annually for twenty
years.

‡ The treaty with the Blackfeet did not contain Article V.

§ These treaties are to be found in the U. S. Statutes at Large, XIV,
see Index.

hundred lodges or families shall have so engaged in agricultural pursuits, they shall be entitled to a farmer and blacksmith, at the expense of the Government, as also teachers, at the option of the Secretary of the Interior."[*]

The treaty with the **Lower Brulé Sioux** provided for locating the band upon a permanent reservation "at or near the mouth of the White river," and promised them Government assistance only when fifty families should engage in agriculture.[†]

The above treaties are an excellent indication of the temper of the Indians at this time. Had the United States felt that its hold upon the Sioux was firm, it would have insisted, to a greater or less degree, upon the essential features of its civilization policy, namely : that the Indians abandon their nomadic life, settle upon permanent reservations, and apply themselves to agriculture. But the Commissioners realized that they entertained no really amicable feeling toward the Government. " At each council complaints were preferred of ill treatment or fraudulent practices by Indian agents, traders, and other white men, and all appeared to regard a restoration of kind relations with the United States in the light of interest or profit to themselves, and not inspired by more humane or generous sentiments."[‡] The attitude of all the Missouri Sioux was exemplified by that of the Minneconjou, of whom the Commissioners

---

* *Ibid.*, 748.

† U. S. Statutes at Large, XIV, 700.

‡ Report of Commission to treat with the Sioux of the Upper Missouri : Report of the Secretary of the Interior, 39th Cong., 1st Sess., 724.

said : " It was deemed useless, as well as impolitic, to make any attempt to enforce conditions upon this wild, nomadic band, having reference to a future location for purposes of agriculture and other labor. The mere mention of a possibility that its members would be compelled eventually to conform to the wishes of the Government in that respect, and thereby consult their own permanent interests, was received with unmistakable tokens of dissent, and the Commission therefore declined to press the point, lest it might endanger the success of the more important object, that of securing * * * peace."*

The treaties of October, 1865, brought about a cessation of hostilities.† During that winter the Indians suffered intensely from cold and hunger, but, notwithstanding the temptation to plunder in order to obtain the necessaries of life, they kept the peace. The summer of 1866, however, found them again in arms. The occasion was this :   In the Fort Laramie treaty of 1851 the Indians had conceded to the Government the right " to establish roads, military and other posts within their respective territories " ;‡ and the Sioux in their treaties of 1865 had confirmed this concession when they agreed " to withdraw from the routes overland already established or hereafter to be established through their country."§ The same treaty of 1851 had established definite boundary lines be-

---

* Report of the Commission to treat with the Sioux of the Upper Missouri : Report of the Secretary of the Interior, 39th Cong., 1st Sess., 722.

† The Minnesota refugees of 1862 and a few other Sioux who had made themselves notorious by murders and depredations upon the whites were still actively hostile but were few in number.

‡ Fort Laramie treaty of 1851 : Copy obtained from the Secretary of the Interior.

§ U. S. Statutes at Large, XIV, 700.

tween the various tribes. The Sioux country included the Black Hills and the Powder River valley, the latter prized by the Indians as an especially rich hunting ground.

Meanwhile gold had been discovered in Montana, and in 1866, the War of the Rebellion being over, immigration began to this Territory. Many of the immigrants went by way of the Powder River valley, and the Indians seriously objected to this use of their favorite hunting ground, as being sure to result in a rapid decrease of game. Nevertheless, in March of 1866 General Pope ordered that military posts be established on this route, and a few months later troops were sent to Forts Phillip Kearney, McPherson, and Reno. The wilder and more independent Sioux were at once aroused, and sent word to the Government that they would not allow the passage of immigrants through the Powder River country nor the establishment of military posts there. The fact that the Government had this same year stopped their annuities due under the treaty of 1851 gave them a pretext for taking up arms. They acknowledged that in that treaty they had granted the United States the right to establish roads and military posts, but they claimed that the United States had lost this right when it ordered their annuities to be discontinued at the end of fifteen instead of fifty years.* Still they would probably have taken no action if the Powder River valley had been left intact. Immigration through this country meant a loss of the means of support, and this they regarded as a sufficient justification for war.

---

* See above, page 96.

The temper of the Sioux had been clearly indicated in the councils at which the treaties of 1865 were made. They had then so strongly expressed their objection to roads through the Powder River valley that the Commissioners had felt called upon to assure them that such roads would probably not be made in the near future. This was unfortunate, for the Indians had demonstrated again and again that they laid as much stress upon spoken as upon written words. It was unfortunate also that the Government persistently closed its eyes to the true state of the case.

Hostilities began in July of 1866, and December 21 Lieutenant Fetterman's party was killed to a man at Fort Phillip Kearney. July 20, 1867, Congress authorized the President to appoint a Commission* to treat with the Indians. This Commission met some of the Sioux at Fort Laramie in the fall of 1867, but Red Cloud refused to be present unless he were assured that the military garrisons in the Powder River valley should be withdrawn. Since he was the leading chief of the hostiles, nothing was accomplished. During the following winter, however, there were no hostilities, and April 29, 1868,† a treaty was negotiated with the Brulé, Ogallala, Minneconjou, Yanktonnais, Uncpapa, Blackfeet, Cuthead, Two Kettle, Sans Arc, and Santee bands of Sioux.

Article II provided that a certain district in Dakota be "set apart for the absolute * * use * * of the Indians herein named, and for such other friendly tribes

---

* The instructions to this Commission are indicative of the governmental policy. See U. S. Statutes at Large, XV, 17.

† U. S. Statutes at Large, XV, 635–40. Ratification advised February 16, 1869 ; proclaimed February 24, 1869.

or individual Indians as from time to time they may be willing, with the consent of the United States, to admit amongst them,"* and for the exclusion from the reservation of all except duly authorized persons.   In this same article the Indians relinquished all claim to any territory in the United States except that to which their right was acknowledged in this treaty.

Article IV provided for the construction of certain buildings.†

Article VI gave to each head of a family the right to select three hundred and twenty acres, and each member of the tribe over eighteen years of age eighty acres, to be the exclusive possession of the person occupying it so long as he should continue to cultivate it.   This same article empowered the "United States to pass such laws on the subject of alienation and descent of property between the Indians and their descendants" as might be thought proper.   It further stipulated that any male Indian over eighteen years of age and party to this treaty, who should settle upon land outside of this reservation and open to Indian occupation, occupy the same for three consecutive years, and make improvements thereon to the value of two hundred dollars, should receive a patent for one hundred and sixty acres and become a citizen of the United States.

Article VII provided for the compulsory education of all children between the ages of six and sixteen years,

---

* U. S. Statutes at Large, XV, 636.

† Such as a warehouse, a storeroom, an agency building, a residence for the physician, and "five other buildings for a carpenter, farmer, blacksmith, miller, and engineer," also a schoolhouse so soon as a sufficient number of children could be induced to attend school.   U. S. Statutes at Large, XV, 636.

and for the erection of a schoolhouse and the employment of a teacher for every thirty of such children.

Article VIII provided that "seeds and argicultural implements for the first year, not exceeding in value one hundred dollars, and for each succeeding year * * * for a period of three years more, * * * not exceeding in value twenty-five dollars,"* should be given to each head of a family who should select land and satisfy the agent that he meant to cultivate it; also that such persons should be instructed by a farmer and receive a second blacksmith when more than one hundred should have begun the cultivation of the soil.

Article X provided for the distribution of certain goods in lieu of annuities under previously existing treaties, for the annual appropriation of ten dollars for each person who should continue to roam and hunt, and twenty dollars for each person who should engage in farming, to be paid in goods; and for the distribution of certain other goods.†

---

* U. S. Statutes at Large, XV, 638.

† " And it is hereby expressly stipulated that each Indian over the age of four years, who shall have removed to and settled permanently upon said reservation and complied with the stipulations of this treaty, shall be entitled to receive from the United States, for the period of four years after he shall have settled upon said reservation, one pound of meat and one pound of flour per day, provided the Indians cannot furnish their own subsistence at an earlier date. * * *

" And it is further expressly stipulated that the United States will furnish and deliver to each lodge of Indians or family of persons legally incorporated with them, who shall remove to the reservation herein described and commence farming, one good American cow and one good well-broken pair of American oxen within sixty days after such lodge or family shall have so settled upon said reservation." U. S. Statutes at Large, XV, 639.

Article XI provided that the tribes party to this agreement "relinquish all right to occupy permanently the territory outside their reservation, * * but yet reserve the right to hunt on any lands north of North Platte and on the Republican Fork of Smoky Hill river so long as the buffalo may range thereon in such numbers as to justify the chase."* The Indians further agreed :

(1) To "withdraw all opposition to the construction of the railroads * * being built on the plains."

(2) To "permit the peaceful construction of any railroad not passing over their reservation."

(3) Not to "attack any persons at home or traveling, nor molest or disturb any wagon trains, coaches, mules, or cattle belonging to the people of the United States or to persons friendly therewith."

(4) Not to "capture or carry off from the settlements white women or children."

(5) Not to "kill or scalp white men, nor attempt to do them harm."

(6) To "withdraw all pretense of opposition to the construction of the railroad * * being built along the Platte river and westward to the Pacific ocean, and * * not in future" to "object to the construction of railroads, wagon roads, mail stations, or other works of utility or necessity which may be ordered or permitted by the laws of the United States," a just indemnity to be paid for those built on the reservation.†

---

* U. S. Statutes at Large, XV, 639.

† "But should such roads or other works be constructed on the lands of their reservation, the Government will pay the tribe whatever amount of damage may be assessed by three disinterested commissioners, to be appointed by the President for that purpose, one of said commissioners to be a chief or head man of the tribe." U. S. Statutes at Large, XV, 639.

(7) To "withdraw all opposition to the military posts or roads * * established south of the North Platte river, or" to "be established, not in violation of treaties heretofore made or hereafter to be made with any of the Indian tribes."

Article XII provided that no treaty for the cession of any portion of the reservation held in common should be valid "unless signed by three-fourths of the adult male population ; and that no cession of the tribe * * be * * construed in such manner as to deprive, without his consent, any individual member of the tribe of his rights to any tract of land selected by him, as provided in Article VI of this treaty."

Article XVI provided " that the country north of the North Platte river and east of the summits of the Big Horn mountains * * be * * considered * * unceded Indian territory ; and * * that no white person * * be permitted to * * occupy any portion of the same or, without the consent of the Indians, * * to pass through the same , and * * that within ninety days after the conclusion of peace with all the bands of the Sioux nation, the military posts* * * established in the territory in this article named * * be abandoned and that the road leading to them and by them to the settlements in * * Montana * * be closed."†

Article XVII provided " that the execution of this treaty * * be construed as * * annulling all treaties and agreements heretofore entered into between the respective parties hereto, so far as such treaties and agree-

* Forts Phillip Kearney, McPherson, and Reno.
† U. S. Statutes at Large, XV, 640.

ments obligate the United States to furnish * * money,
clothing, or articles of property to such Indians * *
as become parties to this treaty, but no farther."*

This treaty marked a decided advance on the part of
the Missouri Sioux.   It was their first step from a wandering to a settled life.   Each individual might still elect
whether he would be a nomad or a farmer, but special
inducements were offered him to be the latter.   The
United States had judged it impracticable to place the
restraints of an agricultural life upon the nation as a
whole, without consulting individual preferences.   There
was need of a gradual transition from barbarism to civilization.   Thus even those who should choose to apply
themselves to agriculture were not wholly debarred from
the pleasures of the chase.   The right to hunt on the

---

* U. S. Statutes at Large, XV, 640.

The articles of this treaty not mentioned in the text were as follows:

Article I provided that peace be maintained, and that offenses
against the Indians on the part of the whites and *vice versa* be punished.

Article III provided that additional arable land be set apart in case
the reservation should not contain enough to allow each authorized person one hundred and sixty acres of land.

Article V provided that the agent reside among the Indians under
his charge and investigate all causes of complaint.

Article IX gave the United States the privilege of withdrawing the
physician, farmer, blacksmith, carpenter, engineer, and miller after ten
years, but bound it, in case of such withdrawal, to pay the Indians an
additional sum of ten thousand dollars annually, to be devoted to educational purposes.

Article XIII provided that physicians, teachers, carpenter, miller,
engineer, farmer, and blacksmiths be furnished the Indians.

Article XIV provided that five hundred dollars annually for three
years from date be expended in presents and distributed to the ten persons who should grow the most valuable crops.

Article XV bound the Indians to consider the agency their home
and to make no permanent settlement elsewhere.   U. S. Statutes at
Large, XV, 635-40.

North Platte and Republican Fork was guaranteed to all, and it is to be presumed that farmer Indians, when not needed at home, might avail themselves of it. On the other hand, the effort to push civilization was apparent in the educational and land-in-severalty clauses, as also in the provision to confer citizenship upon certain Indians who should conform to specified conditions. But the essential element to the civilization of the Sioux was either overlooked or neglected, the reservation assigned to them being largely barren and subject to drought and the blight of the grasshopper. This attempt to force an agricultural life upon barbarians, under circumstances that would have discouraged civilized men, promised little success.

A few of the wilder bands of Sioux were not party to the treaty of 1868. They did not wish to enter into relations with the United States Government because they felt that such action would result in an abridgement of their freedom. These bands, and most notably that of Sitting Bull, formed the nucleus of the hostiles in the war of 1876.

About two-thirds of the treaty Indians settled upon, or at least kept within the limits of, the reservation assigned to them. The remaining third, principally under the leadership of Red Cloud, continued to roam in the region of the Powder River and Big Horn valleys. That they committed some depredations is undoubted, but these were certainly not grave enough to justify General Sheridan's military order of June 29, 1869. It read as follows : " All Indians when on their proper reservations are under the exclusive control and jurisdiction of their agents ; * * * outside the well-defined limits of their reservations they are under the original and exclusive jurisdiction of the military authority, and as a rule will be considered hostile."* This order, although in direct violation of the treaty of 1868, continued in force until December, 1876, and under it Indians exercising the right of chase legally accorded them were again and again hunted down.

The Sioux manifested much uneasiness during the winter of 1869–70. They very much objected to the building of the Northern Pacific Railroad, and did not seem to realize that they had granted this privilege to the United States in Article XI of their late treaty. Moreover, there were rumors abroad that a party was being formed ostensibly to visit the Big Horn mountains, but in reality to explore the Black Hills.† The Chicago *Times* stated that this party would comprise about two thousand men and would be accompanied by three hundred United States soldiers.‡ The Indians were greatly

---

* Report of the Sioux Commission of 1876 : **Report of the** Commissioner of Indian Affairs for 1876, p. 340.

† **These were** within the Sioux reservation.

‡ " Colonel Luke Morrin, Mayor of Cheyenne, is in this city, organizing an expedition to start from Omaha and Cheyenne about the middle of April, to **explore** the Big Horn country, three hundred miles north of Cheyenne. **This** region of territory is known to be rich in mineral and agricultural resources, particularly in gold quartz. The climate is good ; the country is traversed by large rivers ; is well watered, and for farming purposes is unequaled. The object of the expedition is to drive out the Indians and bring the soil under the control of those who will develop its latent treasures. The expedition will comprise about two thousand young men, accompanied by a military escort of three hundred soldiers to be furnished by the Government. All the members of the expedition will be armed and under the control of a military commander, to be chosen by themselves." Extract from Chicago *Times*, February 8, 1870 : Sen. Docs., **41st Cong., 2nd Sess.**, Vol. II, No. 89, p. 2.

excited by these rumors, but Government forbade the
expedition and no serious harm resulted. Shortly afterwards Red Cloud, together with fourteen other chiefs,
visited Washington,* and was so won by his reception
there that he returned home a staunch friend of the
whites. From this time on he exerted his influence for
peace and brought many of the wilder Sioux into closer
connection with the United States, though it cannot be
said that he ever voluntarily advanced the cause of civilization.

During the next few years matters went on smoothly
enough. It is true that whites invaded the Indian country for prospecting and other purposes, and that there
were conflicts between them and the Indians, but there
was no serious trouble. In 1874 the excitement was
greatly increased by a military reconnoitering expedition
under General Custer, which had for its object the exploration of the Black Hills. Gold was found and miners immediately rushed in. The military made a show
of keeping out these unlawful intruders, but it was plain
that their sympathy was with them. The Commissioner
of Indian Affairs for 1875 wrote that soldiers were to be
found in every part of the Sioux reservation, and that
thousands of miners and "pilgrims" were "swarming
over the Sioux country and digging into their sacred
hills for gold." He was able to add that there "had
been no fighting under all this provocation, which five
years" before "would have brought ten thousand paint-

---

* For an account of Red Cloud's visit, with extracts from the daily
papers, see Report of Board of Indian Commissioners for 1870, pp.
38–51.

ed savages into the field for a war which would not have
cost less than fifty millions."*

June, 1875, the Indians of Spotted Tail and Red Cloud
agencies† sold their hunting rights to land in Nebraska,
except a small portion on the Niobrara river, receiving
twenty-five thousand dollars therefor.

In this same month of June a Commission was appointed to treat with the Sioux for the cession of the Black
Hills and the Big Horn country, and three months later
the Commission held a council with them. It was found
impossible, however, to come to terms; the Indians de-
manding more than the Commissioners felt authorized
to pay.‡ That the Sioux entertained an exaggerated no-
tion as to the value of these hills to the United States, is
doubtless true. Their imaginations had been worked
upon by the rapid influx of eager miners. But it is also
true that the hills were of inestimable worth to them.
The region would have best answered their paramount
needs in entering upon their new life. It was the finest
part of their reservation and naturally adapted to agriculture and herding. The fact that the Indians probably did not realize this had no bearing upon the question of a just equivalent for the cession. The Commis-

---

* Report of Commissioner of Indian Affairs for 1875, p. 20.

† For the agreement between these Indians and the United States,
see Report of the Commissioner of Indian Affairs for 1875, p. 179. Commissioners had been appointed in 1873 and in 1874 for the same purpose,
but their negotiations had been unsuccessful. The Indians of the other
agencies were tolerably well settled down and had little practical interest in these hunting grounds. Hence it was not deemed necessary to
make an agreement with them for the relinquishment of their right.

‡ For the report of the Commission, see Report of the Commissioner
of Indian Affairs for 1875, pp. 184-200.

sion, however, did not regard the matter in this light, and advised Congress to take such steps as should force compliance with its demands.

There were at this time a number of Sioux roaming over Western Dakota and Eastern Montana under the leadership of Sitting Bull and other chiefs of less note. These Indians had no treaty relations with the United States Government and desired none. They had strenuously objected to the building of the Northern Pacific Railroad through their hunting grounds, but had committed no organized act of hostility. They had, however, been guilty of various depredations and were regarded as generally unfriendly to the United States. November 9, 1875, E. C. Watkins, United States Indian Inspector, addressed certain complaints against them to the Commissioner of Indian Affairs. After speaking of their defiance of law and authority, he stated that they numbered only a few hundred warriors and advised that troops be sent against them to " whip them into subjection."* On November 27 this letter was transmitted by the Commissioner of Indian Affairs to the Secretary of the Interior,† and two days later by the latter to the Secretary of War.‡ December 3 the Secretary of the Interior sent word to the Secretary of War that he had notified the " Indians that they must remove to a reservation before the 31st day of January next," and that if they neglected to do so they would be regard-

---

* For the letter of E. C. Watkins, United States Indian Inspector, to Hon. E. P. Smith, Commissioner of Indian Affairs, see Ex. Docs., 44th Cong., 1st Sess., Vol. XIV, No. 184, pp. 8–9.

† Ex Docs., 44th Cong., 1st Sess., Vol. XIV, No. 184, p. 7.

‡ *Ibid.*, 10.

ed as hostile and a military force " be sent against them
to compel them to obey the orders of the Indian office."*

A large number of Indians were at this time absent
from the reservation, insufficient appropriations having
compelled many to resort to the chase for subsistence.
The same cause had induced a few to join Sitting Bull.
It was midwinter, and most of these were a long distance
from home. The Sioux Commission of 1876, appointed
to purchase the Black Hills, stated in their report that it
did "not appear that any one of the messengers sent out
by the agents was able to return to his agency by the
time which had been fixed for the return of the Indians."† It is certain that the messenger sent from
Cheyenne river was unable to get back before February
11 ;‡ and he reported that the Indians received the
warning in good spirit and without any exhibition of ill
feeling. They answered that they were hunting buffalo
and could not immediately return, but would visit the
agency early in spring. Other runners also brought information of the friendly disposition of the Indians.§

The state of the case, then, was this : An order was
issued commanding all Sioux Indians off their reservations to return by January 31, 1876.‖ Not sufficient

---

* *Ibid.*, 10.

† Report of the Sioux Commission: Report of the Commissioner of
Indian Affairs for 1876, p. 342.

‡ See letter of H. W. Bingham, United States Indian Agent, to Hon.
J. Q. Smith, Commissioner of Indian Affairs: Ex. Docs., 44 Cong., 1st
Sess., Vol. XIV, p. 26.

§ *Ibid.*, 22.

‖ See Letter of Z. Chandler, Secretary of the Interior, to the Hon. Secretary of War: Ex. Doc., 44th Cong., 1st Sess., Vol. XIV, No. 184, p. 10.

time was allowed the Indians to comply with this order, and promptly on February 1 they were turned over to the War Department.*

The campaign was immediately begun, the first action of importance being the destruction of the village of Crazy Horse made up of friendly "Indians who had separated from Sitting Bull and were on their return to their several agencies."† After this attack inclement weather forced the troops to return to Fort Fetterman, where they remained until May. They then took the field again. June 25 occurred the Battle of the Little Big Horn, which resulted in the complete annihilation of General Custer's five companies. The loss of the Indians has been variously estimated as from forty to one hundred.

Meanwhile Congress had taken action upon the report of the Black Hills Sioux Commission, and, whether upon the spur of its recommendation or not, had passed an act‡

---

* See Letter of Z. Chandler, Secretary of the Interior, to the Hon. Secretary of War: *Ibid.*, 17–18.

† Letter from General **H. H.** Sibley: Eighth Annual Report Board of Indian Commissioners, 21. Rev. Thos. S. Williamson also makes this statement, quoting as his authority Dr. **J.** W. Daniels, Indian Agent and Inspector, and one of the Commissioners of 1876 who obtained the cession of the Black Hills: Minn. **Hist.** Colls., III, 291.

In his report for 1877, p. 15, the Commissioner of Indian Affairs speaks of this camp as hostile, but, since he refers us to the report of the Secretary of War for a detailed account of the campaign, it is to be presumed that he obtained his information from this source. The Secretary of War based his report upon the documents and reports of the generals and their subordinates; and a careful perusal of these brings to light many inconsistencies and inaccuracies.

‡ Indian Appropriation Act, passed August 15, 1876. Quoted in the report of the Sioux Commission: Report of the Commissioner of Indian Affairs for 1876, p. 334.

providing that thereafter no money should be appropriated for the subsistence of these Sioux until they should
relinquish their claim to all land outside their reservation, and should cede that part of their reservation which
lay west of the one hundred and third meridian of longi-
tude. This last embraced the Black Hills country. On
August 24 a Commission was appointed to treat with the
Sioux. The Indians were at this time in sad straits.
Food was scarce* and hunting off the reservation had
been prohibited. They were more keenly aware than
ever of their dependence upon the United States. Under
these circumstances an agreement† was soon reached.
The Sioux made the desired land cession, and consented
to allow three roads to be built westward through their
reservation. In return the Government promised to
issue rations to the Indians until they should become
self-supporting, and to assist them toward civilization by
furnishing them with "schools and instruction in
mechanical and agricultural arts as provided for by the
treaty of 1868."‡ Rations were not to be issued to children between the ages of six and fourteen years who did
not regularly attend school, nor to persons who did not
labor, the sick and infirm excepted. Special provision
was made to aid those who should select land in severalty.§

---

* See Ex. Docs., 44th Cong., 1st Sess., Vol. XIV, No. 184, pp. 58-9.

† See Articles of Agreement: Report of Commissioner of Indian Affairs for 1876, pp. 349-51.

‡ *Ibid.*, 350.

§ " Whenever the head of a family shall in good faith select an allotment of land upon such reservation and engage in the cultivation
thereof, the Government shall, with his aid, erect a comfortable house
on such allotment." Articles of Agreement, Article 6: Report of Commissioner of Indian Affairs for 1876, p. 350.

Some of the tribes agreed to visit the Indian Territory, and, if favorably impressed with the country, to select a permanent home there. This article was made of no effect by a provision in the act of February 28, 1877, prohibiting the removal of any Sioux to the Indian Territory until authorized by Congress.

In the eighth article of the agreement of 1876 the United States had promised to protect the Sioux in their "rights of property, person, and life."* But hardly a month had elapsed before the agency Indians were dismounted and disarmed,† and this despite the fact that the Government had recognized them as friendly and had provided them with such insufficient subsistence as to make recourse to the chase necessary. Some of the ponies were afterwards sold, the Indians receiving the proceeds of the sale in the form of cattle, but the returns were miserably small.‡

Meanwhile the war with the hostiles still continued. In October, 1876, two councils were held with Sitting Bull, but nothing came of them. Soon after some of the Indians surrendered. Sitting Bull and a portion of his following, however, escaped north and crossed over into Canada, the number of these refugees gradually swelling to two hundred lodges. June 20, 1877, the United States was officially notified by the Privy Council of Canada that these Indians were within the British Possessions,

---

    * Articles of Agreement: Report of Commissioner of Indian Affairs for 1876, p. 351.

    † Abridgment of Message and Documents, 1876–77, p. 385; Manypenny, Our Indian Wards, 314–15.

    ‡ The Indians were reimbursed for this loss in 1889. See Report of the Commissioner of Indian Affairs for 1891, p. 138.

and was requested to take such steps as should induce
them, and any others who might "similarly cross the
boundary line, to return to their reserves in the United
States territory."* Accordingly, a Commission was appointed by the President to treat with Sitting. Bull for
his peaceable return, but he and his chiefs declined all
proposals and stated that they wished to remain where
they were. The Canadian authorities warned them that
they could expect no help from Great Britain, and that
crossing the line into the United States would be regarded as an act of hostility by both Governments. The
Indians, however, still adhered to their former decision.†
Thus ended the Sioux war of 1876.‡

The treaty of 1868 had contemplated the ultimate settlement of all the Sioux of the Plains upon the large
reservation. · In 1875 the hunting privilege on the North
Platte and Republican Fork had been surrendered, and
in 1877 the hostile Sioux had either fled to Canada or
submitted to the military. Thus by 1880 all the Missouri Sioux were on the reservation except about four
thousand seven hundred Yanktonnais, who were at Fort
Peck, and one thousand one hundred Northern Sioux,
who had deserted Sitting Bull's camp and were roaming
and hunting just this side of the boundary line between
Canada and the United States.

---

* Quoted in the Report of the Commissioner of Indian Affairs for
1877, p. 17.

† The greater number of these Indians subsequently returned and
proved themselves an element of great disturbance. They were largely
responsible for the Sioux trouble in 1890.

‡ For official documents relating to this war, see Report of the Secretary of War for 1875-6 and 1876-7 : Ex. Docs., 44th Cong., 1st Sess.,
Vol. XIV, No. 184 ; Messages and Documents, 1876-7, 403-417.

It was supposed that, once definitely restricted by reservation limits, the Sioux would apply themselves to agriculture and steadily advance in civilization. The provisions of the treaty of 1868 and those of the agreement of 1876 had looked toward this end. As a matter of fact, however, the Indians made very little progress during the next few years. This was owing to several causes. Sterile soil, drought, and scorching winds made even fair crops a rarity. Moreover, the Indians were given no incentive to work. Government had promised to aid them until they should become self-supporting, and it fulfilled its obligations to the letter, apparently not realizing its duty to help them become self-supporting. It had entirely forgotten that clause in the agreement of 1876, which provided that no rations should be issued to children between the ages of six and fourteen who did not attend school, nor to persons who did not work. Indeed, it failed to provide schools. In 1883 there was not one school among the eight thousand people on Rosebud reserve ;* and during that year Government expended only fourteen thousand eight hundred and ninety-six dollars in the education of these twenty-four thousand three hundred and eighty Sioux.†

The appointment of Indian agents on the spoils system was another serious detriment to the welfare of the Indians. Frequently the agents were unreliable, more frequently still utterly unacquainted with their duties and careless of their responsibilities.

Other causes for the stagnation of the Indians were

---

* Report of the Commissioner of Indian Affairs for 1883, p. 39.

† Compiled from Statistics in the Report of Commissioner of Indian Affairs for 1882, pp. 316-347.

the excitement and restlessness resulting from the war of
1876 and the frequent changes in the location of some of
the agencies, those of Spotted Tail and Red Cloud being
removed some three or four times. By 1880 these
removals had ceased and the Indians then found themselves under the control of six agencies—Standing Rock,
Cheyenne River, Crow Creek, Lower Brulé,* Pine Ridge,
and Rosebud. The condition of the different bands
varied, depending upon the character of the Indians, the
soil and climate, and the agent. But, all told, they had
cultivated only three thousand three hundred and sixty-
four acres and owned only nine thousand four hundred
and forty-four cattle and four hundred and fourteen
swine.† Certainly they had not accomplished much
along two of the main civilizing lines, agriculture and
stock-raising.

Thus far the Sioux had not done very well, but from
1880 to 1890 they made more encouraging progress.
The annual rainfall during the eighties was greater than
usual and crops were correspondingly better. Congress
made increased appropriations for skilled labor. More
and better schools were provided, and competent teachers
employed. At some of the agencies the Indians freighted
the Government supplies and were found efficient and
trustworthy, giving perfect satisfaction to their employ-
ers. This decade also witnessed rapid growth in the
stock-raising industry, the only industry for which much
of the country was fitted. The reforms characteristic of
this period took root here also. Indian police forces and

---

* Crow Creek and Lower Brulé were consolidated August 22, 1882.

† See Table of Statistics, No. 1.

courts of Indian offenses were organized and worked
well ; and the enforcement of the Indian Crimes Act of
1885 helped to maintain order.

There was, however, one source of unrest to the Sioux
during these years. This was the constant agitation
which went on for the reduction of their reservation.
However advisable such a reduction may have been, and
events subsequently proved that it was advisable, it was
unfortunate that agitation concerning a measure to which
the Sioux were so strongly opposed should have continued so long. The Commission* sent to them in 1882
found them little inclined to treat. They stated that
they were perfectly satisfied with the treaty stipulations
under which they were living and desired no change ;
that every agreement with the United States gave them
fewer rights than they had had before. Nevertheless,
some of them signed the agreement presented by the
Commissioners, and this agreement was laid before Congress. At this point the friends of the Indians interposed. They advocated the partition of the Great Sioux
Reservation, but objected to this particular instrument
of partition. They maintained, and with truth, that it
had not been signed by three-fourths of the male adult
population, and that such signatures were necessary according to the treaty of 1868 before that treaty could in
any way be modified ; that the consideration for the cession was inadequate ; that no comprehensive plan had
been outlined for the civilization of the Indians ; and
that unjust and improper means had been used to gain

---

* For the Report of the Commission, together with other documents
pertaining to the same subject, see Sen. Docs., 48th Cong., 1st Sess.,
Vol. IV, No. 70.

their consent.* Accordingly, the bill was not passed. The Commission was instructed to continue negotiations, but it failed to obtain the signatures of the requisite three-fourths.

In 1887 negotiations were renewed. An agreement was drawn up whose terms were decidedly more advantageous to the Indians than those of 1882, but it did not meet their approval. Finally this agreement was amended and presented by a new Commission.† This time a three-fourths vote was obtained, and the agreement‡ was approved by the President March 2, 1889, and became law. The terms were exceedingly liberal. The Sioux ceded to the United States about nine million acres of land. The remainder of the reservation was to be divided into six smaller reserves, and each Indian was to have a claim only to the land in that reserve where he received his rations. Land was to be allotted in severalty according to the Dawes bill of 1887. Thirty schoolhouses were to be immediately erected, and the educational provision of the treaty of 1868 was to continue in force until 1909. Each head of a family or single person over eighteen years of age who should take land in severalty was to be provided "with two milch cows, one pair of oxen, with yoke and chain, or two mares and set of harness in lieu of said oxen, yoke, and chain, * * * one plow, one wagon, one harrow, one hoe, one axe, and

---

* See Fifteenth Annual Report of the Board of Indian Commissioners, 1883, 34–35, 40–41.

† For a full report of the proceedings of this Commission, see Sen. Ex. Docs., 51st Cong., 1st Sess., No. 51, pp. 15–308.

‡ See Report of the Commissioner of Indian Affairs for 1889, pp. 449–458.

one pitchfork, * * * and also fifty dollars in cash."*
The money was to be expended under the direction of
the Secretary of the Interior in aiding such an Indian to
erect a house and other buildings suitable for residence
or in the improvement of his allotment. Three million
dollars were to be given the Sioux as a permanent fund
drawing five per cent. interest, one-half of said interest to
be appropriated for " industrial and other suitable education," and the other half for such purposes, " including
reasonable cash payments per capita," as the Secretary
of the Interior should judge would most contribute to
the advancement of the Indians " in civilization and self-
support." The Secretary of the Interior received discretionary power to expend annually not exceeding ten per
cent. of the principal " in the employment of farmers and
in the purchase of agricultural implements, teams, seeds,"
and " in reasonable cash payments." The remainder of
the fund was to be expended for the Indians at the end
of fifty years in such manner as Congress should determine.

The terms of this agreement were most generous, and
it seemed as though their fulfillment must insure a decided advance on the part of the Sioux. The size of the
reservation had been an impediment to the civilization
of the Indians, as well as a hindrance to the spread of the
whites. The Sioux had been shut in by themselves, had
lacked stimulating contact with a civilized population. It
was a well known fact that the Yanktonnais at Crow
Creek, who were not thus isolated from our people, made

---

* Report of the Commissioner of Indian Affairs for 1889, pp. 454-5.

more rapid progress than their kinsmen nearer the center of the great Reservation.*

The fifteen years preceding this agreement had witnessed the steady development of two distinct parties among the Sioux. There were those who adapted themselves to the new order and gradually acquired, at least to some extent, the habits and customs of civilized life. These formed the nucleus of the progressive party in whose ranks were to be found nearly all who had been Christianized and who were really friendly to the United States. Opposed to these were those who clung to the old order and who resisted every advance of civilization. These were antagonistic to every innovation, and awaited only an occasion to display their hatred of the Government. It was inevitable that there should be these two parties. Hardly twenty years had passed since these Indians had roamed the plains at will and subsisted almost entirely by the chase. Only those who possessed most adaptability could adjust themselves in so short a time to the new environment. The existence of this pagan party was, therefore, most natural, but the fact does not exonerate the Government from blame; it should have made provision to control it. The lack of foresight on the part of the United States was largely responsible for the so-called "outbreak" of 1890.

The cession of 1889, despite the liberal compensation, had not been favored by all the Sioux. There was a small minority that had bitterly opposed it. Even those who had signed the agreement had relinquished nine million acres of land with some reluctance. They doubtless

---

* This may be seen from a careful comparison of the civilization statistics in the reports of the Commissioner of Indian Affairs.

realized that a more determined effort was to be made to civilize them, and they felt a vague unrest as to the future. This was accentuated by the partial failure of crops in 1889 and in 1890,* and great mortality resulting from the grippe, measles, and whooping-cough. The Indians said their children were all dying from diseases introduced by the whites.

This state of affairs made it particularly unfortunate that the issue of rations should have been cut down at this time. While negotiations for the cession were pending, the Indians had asked again and again whether the new agreement would result in their receiving less rations, and had been assured that it would not.† Yet large reductions in beef were made at the various agencies, amounting at Rosebud to two million and at Pine Ridge to one million pounds. Moreover, various provisions in the agreement were not promptly fulfilled, among them those providing for appropriations for education and for the payment for the ponies taken in 1876–7. Besides

---

* In addition to this partial failure, the crops at Pine Ridge were trampled down or eaten by cattle which had broken into the fields while the Indians were at the agency treating with the Commissioners. Report of Commissioner of Indian Affairs for 1891, I, 133; *Scribner's Magazine*, April, 1891, 446.

† I cannot do better than quote the words of the Commission on this point: "During our conference at the different agencies we were repeatedly asked whether the acceptance or rejection of the act of Congress would influence the action of the Government with reference to their rations, and in every instance the Indians were assured that subsistence was furnished in accordance with former treaties, and that signing would not affect their rations, and that they would continue to receive them as provided in former treaties. Without our assurances to this effect it would have been impossible to have secured their consent to the cession of lands." Report and Proceedings of the Sioux Commission: Sen. Ex. Docs., 51st Cong., 1st Sess., No. 51, p. 23.

these, there were other causes which added to the gloom
and misfortune of the Indians.*

Matters were in this critical state when the report of a
Messiah spread among the Sioux.† It was said that he
had declared that their term of humiliation and punishment was at an end ; that they were now to become the
dominant race upon the continent, and were to avenge
the wrongs which had been heaped upon them by the
whites. Their dead were to be raised up and their
ponies and hunting grounds restored. It was enjoined
upon all who believed in the Messiah to show their faith
in him by repeated "ghost dances," each dance to be
prolonged until the strength of the dancer was exhausted, or he swooned.

This strange delusion immediately laid hold of some
of the non-progressive Indians that were superstitious
enough to believe it. Others became converts because

---

* The disease of blackleg had appeared among the cattle in 1888.
The agreement of 1889 had changed the boundary line between Pine
Ridge and Rosebud, and some of the Indians at the latter reserve had
been obliged to change their location. This caused a certain amount of
discomfort. The census of the Indians had revealed the fact that their
number was decidedly less than that upon which the issue of rations
was based, and this meant a diminution of rations. Report of Commissioner of Indian Affairs for 1891, I, 133–4.

† It did not originate with them. According to Rev. W. J. Cleve-
land, who made an extended investigation into the matter, the Indians
said that the report came "from the people who wear rabbit-skin blankets, * * * far west of the Yellow Skins, who are far west of the
Utes." Mr. Herbert Welsh thinks that by these may be meant the
Pueblo Indians of New Mexico and Arizona because, I quote his words,
"they wear rabbit-skin blankets, live far west of the Utes, and, moreover, hold the old Aztec tradition of Montezuma, their Savior, returning to free their race." The Meaning of the Dakota Outbreak: *Scribner's Magazine*, April, 1891, p. 446.

they felt that in so doing they might find an opportunity to throw off the fetters of civilization. But the number of those influenced would probably have been very small had it not been for the Sitting Bull faction. This was largely made up of those who had fled to Canada in the war of 1876, had returned four or five years later, and were now at Standing Rock. Sitting Bull himself was the chief mischief-maker, and it was largely through his efforts that the craze gained a firm footing at his agency.

Meanwhile the excitement laid hold of the Sioux at Pine Ridge, Rosebud, and Cheyenne River, though there were fewer converts than at Standing Rock. Ghost dances became frequent; industrial occupations were neglected, and a general demoralization ensued. Matters grew worse as the summer advanced. Sitting Bull's runners were active, hurrying here and there, rousing this and that band, and always appealing to the lowest and most ignorant.

As early as June, 1890, there had been rumors afloat that the Sioux were secretly planning to rise, but the reports of the Indian agents indicated that there were no grounds for apprehending serious trouble. The probability of an outbreak grew with the increase of disturbance during the summer and early autumn, and in November the attitude of some of the Indians was decidedly unfriendly. The agents at Pine Ridge, Rosebud, and Cheyenne River reported that the Sioux were arming, and November 13 the Indian Office recommended that the matter be submitted to the War Department. The action of this department was precipitated by a telegram* from Agent Royer of Pine Ridge, dated November 15.

---

* See Report of Commissioner of Indian Affairs for 1891, I, 128.

The telegram seems to have been prompted by no special exigency.   Agent Royer stated that the Indians were "wild and crazy" and were dancing in the snow ; and that the employees and Government property were without protection.   He urged that the leaders be arrested at once.   Five days later a military force of five companies of infantry and three troops of cavalry arrived at Pine Ridge.   Troops were ordered to other Sioux agencies also.   When the detachment sent to Rosebud reached that reservation, "about one thousand Indians—men, women, and children—stampeded toward Pine Ridge and the bad lands, destroying their own property before leaving, and that of others en route."*

During this time Sitting Bull's camp at Grand River, forty miles from Standing Rock agency, had been the center of great disturbance.   December 15 he was arrested by a force of Indian police.   "He agreed to accompany them to the agency, but while dressing caused considerable delay, and during this time his followers began to congregate to the number of one hundred and fifty, so that when he was brought out of the house they had the police entirely surrounded.   Sitting Bull then refused to go and called upon his friends, the ghost dancers, to rescue him.   At this juncture one of them shot Lieutenant Bullhead.   The lieutenant then shot Sitting Bull, who also received another shot and was killed outright.   Another shot struck Sergeant Shavehead and then the firing became general.   In about two hours the police had secured possession of Sitting Bull's house and driven their assailants into the woods."†

---

* Report of the Commissioner of Indian Affairs for 1891, I, 128.

† Report of Commissioner of Indian Affairs for 1891, I, 129.

Meanwhile "groups of Indians from the different reservations had commenced concentrating in the 'bad lands' upon or in the vicinity of the Pine Ridge reservation. Killing of cattle and destruction of other property by these Indians almost entirely within the limits of Pine Ridge and Rosebud reservations occurred, but no signal fires were built, no warlike demonstrations were made, no violence was done to any white settler, nor was there cohesion or organization among the Indians themselves. Many of them were friendly Indians who had never participated in the ghost dance but had fled thither from fear of soldiers, * * or through over-persuasion of friends. The military gradually began to close in around them, and they offered no resistance, and a speedy and quiet capitulation of all was confidently expected."*

Among these Indians was Big Foot's band. This left the bad lands and started toward Pine Ridge agency, and meeting our troops proposed a parley with them. Upon being refused they surrendered unconditionally, but turned over to the military very few arms. Their teepees were searched and sixty guns were found. A detachment of troops was then ordered to take the arms from their persons, and while this was going on a shot was fired.† "A short, sharp, indiscriminate fight immediately followed, and, during the fighting and the subsequent flight and pursuit of the Indians, the troops lost twenty-five killed and thirty-five wounded, and of the Indians, eighty-four men and boys, forty-four women,

---

* Report of Commissioner of Indian Affairs for 1891, I, 130.

† Probably by a crazy Indian.

and eighteen children were killed, and at least thirty-three were wounded, many of them fatally."[*] The fact that so many women and children were killed speaks ill for our soldiers. According to the Indian account[†] these women and children were indiscriminately massacred even under the flag of truce ; and there is reason to believe that there is some truth in this assertion.

The result of the fight at Wounded Knee Creek was a further concentration of the Indians upon the bad lands, and January 6, 1891, Major-General Schofield ordered that army officers be assigned to the Sioux agencies to exercise " military supervision and control," but " without interfering unnecessarily with the administration of the agents of the Indian Bureau."[‡] During the next few weeks there were some skirmishes, but in less than a month the Indians had returned to their agencies and all serious trouble was practically over.[§]

Shortly after a Commission from the Sioux visited Washington and were given an opportunity to state their grievances. The difficulties were for the most part settled by the Indian appropriations made in the acts of

---

[*] Report of Commissioner of Indian Affairs for 1891, I, 130.

[†] For the Indian account of the fight at Wounded Knee Creek, see Report of the Commissioner of Indian Affairs for 1891, I, Appendix, pp. 179–181. This account, although given wholly from the Indian stand-point and, therefore, probably a little one-sided, bears the stamp of sincerity.

[‡] Report of Commissioner of Indian Affairs for 1891, I, 131.

[§] For a full and most excellent account of this so-called Sioux " outbreak," see Report of the Commissioner of Indian Affairs for 1891, I, pp. 123–142.

January 19* and March 3, 1891.† Congress had then complied with all its treaty stipulations, and fulfilled the promises made by the Sioux Commission of 1889, except that it had not provided for the one hundred and eighty-seven thousand and thirty-nine dollars which the Commission had advised should be paid the Crow Creek Indians because the per capita amount of land on their reserve was less than that on the others, being only two hundred and sixty acres.‡

It has seemed necessary to dwell at some length upon this so-called "outbreak" of 1890, because its nature was characteristic of the temper and condition of the Indians. The first point to be noted is the fact that the Sioux were no longer a united people. Their experiences of the last twenty years had broken tribal relations and community of interests. A sense of individual responsibility and personal independence had begun to dawn upon them. This was illustrated in the sharp distinction between the progressive and non-progressive parties. Furthermore, the great body of the Sioux were friendly to the Government. Under circumstances which they would once have eagerly seized upon as an excuse to take up arms, they remained peaceful and quiet. It is probably true that a small party under the leadership of

---

* See U. S. Statutes at Large, XXVI, 720.

† See *ibid.*, 1001-2.

‡ The Crow Creek and Lower Brulé Indians numbered the same, yet the latter received one hundred and eighty-seven thousand and thirty-nine acres more than the former. Hence the Commission urged the former should be given one hundred and eighty-seven thousand and thirty-nine dollars, that is one dollar for each acre which in justice they should have received but did not. Report and Proceedings of the Sioux Commission : Sen. Ex. Docs., 51st Cong., 1st Sess., No. 51, pp. 30-1.

Sitting Bull and others were preparing to break away from their treaty relations in the spring, but this was made up largely of the wilder element which had come into the reservation during the last decade and had not yet adjusted itself to the new environment.

Altogether, considering the unsettled condition of the Indians consequent upon the rapid changes in their life during the preceding thirty years, the unfortunate circumstances which combined to make them hopeless and despondent, and the peculiar temptations which befell them to revert back to the old savage life—considering these things, the wonder is not that there was an outbreak in 1890, but that the proportions which it assumed were so small. This must afford encouragement rather than discouragement as to the ultimate solution of the Sioux problem. The fact that progress has been made proves capacity therefor. It remains now to surround this capacity by such conditions as will cause it to bear fruit.

CHAPTER V.

The division of the great Sioux family into the Sioux of the Mississippi and the Sioux of the Plains was made on the basis of their geographical location. That for a time this location determined the attitude of the Indians toward the Government, and of the Government toward the Indians, is apparent on the surface. The Mississippi Sioux were settled upon reservations and brought to an agricultural life sooner than the Missouri Sioux, simply because they came in contact with our civilization earlier. Not until our frontiers had pushed themselves further westward were the Sioux of the Plains brought into close relationship with the United States. The Yanktons, as being the most easterly band of these wilder Indians, were the first to be influenced by our civilization policy. Their history, from 1858 on, is so entirely separate from that of their kinsmen that it has seemed best to give it a separate chapter.

In the year 1851 the Sisseton, Wahpeton, Mdewakan-tonwan, and Wahpekute bands had ceded a large territory to the United States. The Yanktons insisted that this territory had in part belonged to them, and that their right to it should have been recognized in this treaty; and they made themselves especially troublesome whenever the annuities were paid. Finally, February 19, 1858, the Government made a treaty* with them.

---

* U. S. Statutes at Large, XI, 743-9.

Article I provided that the Yanktons cede all their
lands to the United States except four hundred thousand
acres in the southeastern part of Dakota,* to be set aside
as a reservation for them.

Article II defined the boundaries of the land ceded.

Article III gave the United States the right to construct roads across the reservation, a fair equivalent to
be paid for land so used.†

Article IV provided that the United States protect the
Indians in the peaceable enjoyment of their reservation ;
and pay them annually $65,000 for the first ten years,
$40,000 for the next ten years, $25,000 for the next ten
years, and $15,000 for the next twenty years, the Secre-
tary of the Interior to be given discretionary power over
the expenditure of this money, and the annuities to be
discontinued if the Indians should not make "reasonable
and satisfactory efforts to advance and improve their
condition."‡ The United States further promised to pay
the Indians $25,000 to maintain them during the first
year after their removal and to assist them in beginning
an agricultural life ; to spend $10,000 for educational
purposes, the Indians to send all their children between
the ages of seven and eighteen to school, and those not
doing so to be deprived of a portion of their annuities ;
and to erect "a mill suitable for grinding grain and-

---

* " Beginning at the mouth of the Naw-izi-wa-koo-pah or Chonteau
river ; thence down said river to the place of beginning, so as to include
the said quantity of four hundred thousand acres."   U. S. Statutes at
Large, XI, 744.

† This same article provided that the Yanktons remove to their
reservation within a year from the date of the treaty.

‡ U. S. Statutes at Large, XI, 745.

sawing timber,"* and make other improvements not exceeding in value $15,000.

Article V bound the Indians not to destroy any of the improvements made by the Government, and, in case of such destruction, to pay for the same with their annuities.

Article VI empowered the chiefs and headmen in open council to authorize a certain portion of their annuities, not exceeding in the aggregate $150,000, to be paid to satisfy their just debts, and to provide for such of their half-breeds as did not live upon the reservation or draw annuities ; not more than $15,000 to be used for this purpose in one year.

Article VIII provided that the Yanktons be secured in the free use of so much of the Red Pipestone quarry as they had been accustomed to frequent for the purpose of securing stone for pipes.

Article IX gave the United States the right to establish " military posts, roads, and Indian agencies "† upon the reservation, due compensation to be made for any injury to the property of the Yanktons.

Article X provided for the exclusion of all but duly authorized persons from the reservation, and prohibited the Indians from disposing of any of their land except to the United States. The Secretary of the Interior was given discretionary power to cause the reservation to be surveyed and allotted, each head of a family or single person to receive a separate farm, with such rights of possession as the Secretary might deem just.

Article XII provided that annuities be withheld from those who should drink intoxicating liquors or procure

* U. S. Statutes at Large, XI, 746.
† U. S. Statutes at Large, XI, 746.

them for others, and from those who should in any way violate the terms of the treaty.

Article XIV provided that the United States be free from all obligations toward the Yanktons except those under this treaty and the Fort Laramie treaty of 1851.*

The reservation upon which the Yanktons were settled contained about ninety-five per cent. of good, arable land especially adapted to wheat-raising ; the remainder was suitable for pasture. There was, however, always the chance that the crops would be eaten or destroyed by grasshoppers. The Indians showed themselves possessed of a good deal of adaptability. They at once settled down upon their reservation and made an auspicious beginning in their new life. Their annuities were small, but for the first few years they supported themselves easily by farming and hunting. Throughout the war of 1862 they remained loyal to the Government, and furnished

---

* Article VII provided that certain persons who had been of service to the Yanktons receive allotments upon the ceded lands.

Article XI provided that the Yanktons commit no depredations, preserve peaceful relations with other tribes and with the United States, and deliver to the proper Government officers " all offenders against the treaties, laws, or regulations of the United States."

Article XIII provided that no part of the annuities be taken to satisfy claims except those named in this treaty, or those which might arise under it, or under the trade and intercourse laws.

Article XV provided that an agent be appointed for the Yanktons.

Article XVI provided that the expenses of making this treaty and of surveying the reservation and the Red Pipestone quarry be borne by the United States.

Article XVII provided that this treaty be binding as soon as ratified by the Senate and the President.

fifty scouts* who did us most excellent service. Until
1864 the Yanktons progressed rapidly, but for nearly a
decade of years after that they were in a miserable state.
The Government either failed to keep its treaty promises
or administered the affairs of the Indians so badly that
it amounted to the same thing.† Their agency buildings
were in a dilapidated condition ; their crops repeatedly
failed, either because not planted in time or because destroyed by the grasshoppers ; they suffered from the spo-
liations of the soldiers, and the Government delayed
paying the ten thousand dollars which Congress had
appropriated as indemnity.

With the early seventies came a change for the better.
The United States assisted the tribe with liberal appro-
priations.   The Episcopal Church and the American
Board of Commissioners for Foreign Missions did good

---

* These scouts received no compensation but arms, ammunition,
clothing, and rations until thirty years later, when, by the agreement of
December 31, 1892, they were awarded $225 each. See Report of Com-
missioner of Indian Affairs for 1894, p. 448.

† " Agent Conger found the Yanctons in a very unsatisfactory condition and expressing much discontentment, and complaining that the
Government had not kept its promises to them. * * * He reported the
agency buildings in a dilapidated condition, and everything run down ;
no cattle or stock, farming tools few and in bad condition, and very
small preparation for a crop this year. * * * There is no school on
the reservation, and none has been in existence, although the treaty provides liberally for one, and the vouchers of late Agent Burleigh are on
file for the expenditure of considerable sums of money for the purpose."
Report of Commissioner of Indian Affairs for 1865–6 : Report of the
Secretary of the Interior, 39th Cong., 1st Sess., 194.

Being advised of the condition of the Yanktons, Congress ordered
special inquiry to be made into their matters and a report thereon. This
report I have been unable to find, but it seems certain that it resulted in
a better administration of the Yankton affairs.

work. Sheep and cattle-raising **were** introduced, and material prosperity increased. After **a time** a court of Indian offenses was established and Indian police **were** put on duty. When the Land in Severalty Bill was passed, the Yankton reservation was one **of the** first made subject **to** its action. 167,324.12 acres **were allotted to 1,484** Indians, and 851.88 acres **reserved** for agency, church, **and** school purposes. Under the act of February 28, 1891, which provided that all members of a tribe have equal amounts of land, **1,128 more allotments, embracing** 96,762 acres, were made. **About one-half of these were** additions to those made under **the Land in Severalty Bill.**

The surplus lands of this reservation amounted to 167,- 303 acres. Under the provisions **of the** act of 1887, **a Com-mittee was appointed** October 1, 1892, to negotiate with the **Yanktons for the** sale **of** this unallotted land. The first **agreement** presented by the Commissioners provided that Government **cause** "the land to be appraised under certain restrictions, and **sold to the** highest bidder, who also must be an actual settler." * **The** land **was** not to be **sold at less than the appraised** value ; and **the proceeds** of the sale **were** to become a permanent fund whose annual interest should be distributed among the members of the tribe. The Indians favored this proposition, but before action could be taken **upon it** a disagreement arose among the Commissioners, as a result of which one **of** them resigned. The appraisement plan was then laid aside, **and a new** agreement **drawn** up. This provided for the cession of the surplus lands **for the** gross sum of **six** hundred thousand dollars, **equal to** about three

* Report of E. W. Foster, **Yankton Agent: Report of the Commis-** sioner of Indian Affairs for 1893, **p. 312.**

dollars and sixty cents per acre. There was decided opposition to the second agreement, especially among the more intelligent Indians. They said that land in their near neighborhood was valued at ten dollars and twenty dollars per acre, and that their own was worth quite as much ; but that they would sell on the appraisement plan, and only on that plan, fixing the minimum price at six dollars per acre.* "The Commissioners, however, were determined to make a success of their undertaking, and, when the opposition showed strength, they became liberal in expending money. They employed a small army of interpreters, couriers, and messengers. Councils were called, harangues made, and feasts given."† In this way enough signatures were obtained,

---

* "Gentlemen," said they, "you have a wrong conception of our rights on this reservation. You seem to regard our title to this land as parallel to that of the Western Sioux to the Great Sioux reservation recently ceded. Their title was simply the right of occupancy. Ours is a title in fee; it is the solemn pledge of the Government to protect this tribe in the peaceable possession of this land as a home forever. Now, although we have accepted allotments in severalty, and a considerable body of land is left unallotted, yet we are not compelled to sell it at less than it is worth. Wild land adjoining the reservation of similar character sells from ten dollars to twenty dollars per acre. We believe that fifty thousand acres of our land would sell on an unrestricted market for twenty dollars per acre. We believe that within the next ten years our lands will sell for twenty-five dollars to fifty dollars per acre. Now we believe that it would be for the best interests of this tribe to sell these surplus lands at a fair price so that we can have white people for our near neighbors, and therefore we will agree to cede our lands on the plan you first proposed, fixing the minimum price at six dollars per acre, but otherwise we shall oppose a sale." Quoted in Report of E. W. Foster, United States Indian Agent at Yankton: Report of Commissioner of Indian Affairs for 1893, p. 311.

† Report of E. W. Foster, United States Indian Agent: Report of the Commissioner of Indian Affairs for 1893, p. 311.

but the worth of some of them may be judged from the following words of Agent Foster : " Since then those whose names were attached to the document have asked me many times what their names are signed to, and many of those who refused to sign have desired me to ascertain the terms of the agreement they declined to sign ; but as no copy of it was left here, and as it was never read in open meeting but once, and was kept closely sealed from the public, I have not been able to make any satisfactory explanation."*

When the report of the Commissioner of Indian Affairs for 1893 was written this agreement was still on file with the Secretary of the Interior, and no action had been taken for its transmittal to Congress.† In addition to the six hundred thousand dollars to be paid the tribe for the cession, the agreement provided that twenty dollars be paid each adult male.

The Yanktons may now be reckoned among the civilized communities of the United States. For the most part they wear citizens' clothes and live in houses ; they own their land in fee simple and are fairly successful in cultivating it ; they have churches and schools ; finally, they are citizens. But there are still dangers ahead of them, and the greatest are those that have to do with the much mooted question of law. Their agent writes that " their relationship with local State authorities has not changed. The reservation has been within an organized county for many years, yet the county authorities decline to recognize the Indians or any of the residents of the

---

* Report of E. W. Foster, United States Indian Agent : Report of the Commissioner of Indian Affairs for 1893, p. 311.

† Since then the agreement has been ratified. See Report of the Commissioner of Indian Affairs for 1894, 444–450.

reserve as entitled to the rights and privileges of citizenship. The Constitution of the State of South Dakota
expressly disclaims any right or title to any lands owned
or held by an Indian or Indian tribe that are exempt
from taxation, and this is held to disclaim any jurisdiction over the acts, either civil or criminal, of the residents
within an Indian country."* Thus the Yanktons, as
indeed the rest of our Indian citizens, are still hampered
in their development by the lack of proper State legislation.

---

* Report of E. W. Foster, United States Indian Agent at Yankton :
Report of the Commissioner of Indian Affairs for 1893, p. 307.   .

CHAPTER VI.

STATUS OF THE SIOUX IN 1893.

In 1893 the Sioux were under the supervision of ten agencies.* At all of these the Indians were leading a more or less settled life, and, except for those at Fort Peck, had begun to partially support themselves. Progress had been most marked at Sisseton, Santee, Yankton, and Devil's Lake agencies, and for several reasons. These Indians were the first to leave off their nomadic life and to settle down to agriculture.† The reservations upon which they had been placed had been of fairly good character ; the soil was rich and fertile and repaid the toil of cultivation, though the crops were sometimes ruined by drought and parching winds. The Indians at these agencies lived in houses and had largely adopted the habits and customs of civilized life ; all, with the exception of a few at Devil's Lake, had received allotments

---

* See second map. Besides these there was a small band of Mdewakantonwan Sioux in Minnesota, not living upon a reservation and having no treaty relations with the Government. In various Indian appropriation acts the aggregate sum of fifty-eight thousand dollars had been set aside for these Indians, and October 16, 1886, a special agent was appointed to purchase lands for them. See Report of Commissioner of Indian Affairs for 1891, I, 110–2.

† The Yanktons did not settle down until 1858, but that was ten years before the other Sioux of the Plains were placed upon a reservation.

Sisseton and Santee reservations had been thrown open to settlement under the Homestead Law.

in severalty and were citizens of the United States. This
as yet meant little to them, since they had not thus far
been educated to an appreciation of their obligations and
privileges. With the Sioux at Flandreau,* under the
control of the Santee agency, it was otherwise. Their
agent spoke of them as sober, steady, industrious, and
law-abiding. They were, moreover, the only Sioux who
were entirely self-supporting.

The Crow Creek and Lower Brulé Indians were in a
stage intermediate between the above and the so-called
Sioux of the Plains. They were not quite so far advanced
as the Mississippi Sioux, but were making rapid
progress. Four hundred and ninety families were living
upon and cultivating allotments in severalty. A large
proportion were engaged in agriculture and stock-raising.
The uncertainty of the climate inclined the Indians to
the latter. Nearly all wore citizen's dress.

The rest of the Sioux of the Plains were on Pine Ridge,
Rosebud, Standing Rock, Cheyenne River, and Fort Peck
reservations. They had made little progress since 1868,
a fact to be attributed partially to the utter unfitness of
their lands for agriculture. The Indian Appropriation
Act of 1893 made provision for the sinking of an artesian
well at Rosebud, one at Standing Rock, and one at Pine
Ridge, these wells to be used for irrigating purposes.
They were, however, still of the future. The Indians
were devoting themselves to stock-raising and were making some advance along this line. Fifty-six allotments

---

* These, it will be remembered, had taken up homesteads under the
sixth article of the treaty of 1868. This would seem to indicate that they
were more enterprising than most of their kinsmen. They had, moreover, been citizens for about twenty years.

had been made at Rosebud, but none elsewhere. The Fort Peck* Indians stood lowest in civilization.

According to the statistics of the Report of the Commissioner of Indian Affairs for 1893, the Sioux numbered twenty-four thousand nine hundred and seventy-one. There were one thousand nine hundred and ninety living upon and cultivating allotments in severalty. There were seventy-eight schools upon the reservations, with an average attendance of three thousand two hundred and forty-two children. The support of these schools cost the Government $371,615.16, and other parties $49,-768.72. Thus $421,383.88 were spent for the education of the Sioux during this year. Despite the above figures,† which are certainly hopeful, it may be questioned whether the Government did its utmost for the Indians. It failed to enforce compulsory attendance. Many of the Indians do not see that education is absolutely necessary in order that they may become fitted for citizenship. Neither do they understand its relation to the question of self-support. Their annuities will cease and they will then have to care for themselves unless the United States should voluntarily assist them. This the Government is not bound to do. But it has a duty in another direction. It must educate the Indians to an appreciation of their true condition, and this must be done largely through schools. While, therefore, the school report of the Sioux for 1893 is encouraging, it is not all that could be wished. The enforcement of compulsory attendance, and larger

---

* These Indians have not been treated in this paper. A history of their relations with the United States Government would be simply another illustration of the principles already brought out.

† See Tables of Statistics, numbers 3 and 4.

appropriations for the accommodation of the additional pupils that will thus be secured, are necessary. This, together with civil service reform, will smooth the path which the Indians must tread to ultimate competition with the whites. The Sioux are a brave people, and superior to most of their race in mental ability. In the midst of a proper environment there is no reason why they should not ultimately become intelligent and self-supporting citizens. Their future, together with that of the other Indian tribes, will depend largely upon the Government's conscientious performance of duty toward them. The attitude of the American people, as reflected in Congress, will determine the solution of the Indian problem.

TABLE No. 1.

*Statistics relating to Indian Schools among the Sioux.**

Name of Agency.	Number of Schools	Average Attendance	Amount Expended in Education	
			By Government	By Religious Societies
Standing River.........	3	90	$6,460	**$1,500**
Cheyenne River	5	81		5,420
Crow Creek... .. ..,	1	28		
Lower Brulé............	4	36		
Rosebud...............	1	23	430	350
Pine Ridge..	3	59	1,080	280

* Compiled from the Report of the Commissioner of Indian Affairs for 1880.

TABLE No. 2.

Statistics relating to the Civilization of the Sioux as seen in the Cultivation and Allotment of Land and the Amount of Stock Owned.*

Name of Agency	Name of Tribe	Population	Number of Acres				Allotments in Severalty	Horses	Mules	Cattle	Swine
			In Reservation	Tillable	Cultivated by Govern't	Cultivated by Indians					
Standing River	Lower Yanktonnais	852	31,408,551 †	25,000		576	77	850	7	2,600	15
	Upper "	488									
	Uncpapa	521									
	Blackfeet	720									
Cheyenne River	Two Kettle	680									
	Sans Arc	322									
	Minneconjou	523									
	Blackfeet	229									
Crow Creek	Lower Yanktonnais	969	630,312	400,000	143	211	27	410	5	384	64
Lower Brulé	Lower Brulé	1,300		64,000	60	322		2,400	2	800	45
Rosebud	Northern Brulé	3,566			40	455		4,000	102	2,150	80
	Loafer	1,564									
	Wahzahzah	1,164									
	Mixed Sioux	1,020									
Pine Ridge	Sioux	7,200				1,800		5,000	250	3,510	210

* Compiled from the Report of the Commissioner of Indian Affairs for 1893.

† Include all but Crow Creek Indians.

TABLE No. 3.

*Statistics relating to the Civilization of the Sioux as seen in the Cultivation and Allotment of Land and the Amount of Stock Owned.**

Name of Agency	Name of Tribe	Population	Number of acres cultivated during the year by Indians	Families actually living upon and cultivating allotments in severalty	Stock Owned by Indians				
					Horses and Mules	Cattle	Swine	Sheep	Domestic Fowls
Devil's Lake	Sioux	1,063	3,500	290	570	479			250
Sisseton and Wahpeton	Sisseton Wahpeton	1,851	5,247	347	1,126	207		30	3,839
Yankton	Yankton	1,730	4,307	550	1,658	1,819	416	53	4,329
Santee	Santee	960	4,590	200	602	325	300	4	1,800
	Santee Sioux of Flandreau	310	1,110	57	200	300	40	20	2,000
Crow Creek and Lower Brulé	Lower Yanktonnais	1,655	3,250	290	1,084	1,728			901
	Lower Brulé	1,012	1,250	200	1,056	2,600			100
Pine Ridge	Sioux	5,188	†4,680		†10,774	17,960	†24		†1,000
Rosebud	Brulé, Loafer, Wahzalzah, Two Kettle, Northern Bands	4,276	3,743	56	4,763	12,991	210	22	2,017
Standing Rock	Sioux	3,833	5,000		3,522	9,673	163		7,877
Forest City	Blackfeet, Minneconjou, Sans Arc, Two Kettle	†2,417	†1,703		†4,521	†7,260	†24		†1,820
Fort Peck	Yanktonnais	1,287	§450		§1,640	§1,227			§500
		24,972		1,990					

* Compiled from the Report of the Commissioner of Indian Affairs for 1893.
† Computed on the basis of the entire population, one-sixth of whom are not Sioux.
‡ Taken from Report of 1892.
§ Computed on basis of the entire population, one-third of whom are Assinaboine.

TABLE No. 4.

Statistics relating to Schools among the Sioux during the Year ending June 30, 1893.

Name of Agency	Number of Schools		Average Attendance		Cost to Government	Cost to Other Parties
	Boarding	Day	Boarding	Day		
Devil's Lake	2	3	358	52	$56,473.61	$3,100.00
Sisseton and Wahpeton ..	2		134		23,452.59	6,372.64
Yankton.	2		142		22,108.11	3,600.00
Santee..	3	1	282	35	87,764.17	13,435.63
Crow Creek and Lower Brulé..	4		319		45,694.00	4,291.45
Pine Ridge	2	20	232	478	49,006.64	
Rosebud.. ..	2	15	141	390	26,005.52	12,500.00
Standing Rock...	3	8	218	199	35,448.87	3,000.00
Forest City.... .	4	6	135	100	23,412.62	3,469.00
Fort Peck.....	1		27		2,249.03	
	25	53	1,988	1,254	$371,615.16	$49,768.72

* Compiled from the Report of the Commissioner of Indian Affairs for 1893.

BIBLIOGRAPHICAL INDEX.

Adams, Henry. History of the United States of America, 1801–1817. 9 vols. New York, 1890–1.

Annals of Congress, 1789–1824. 42 vols. Washington.

Benton, Thomas H. Thirty Years in the United States Senate. 2 vols. New York, 1854.

Bluewater, Battle of. Senate Executive Documents, 34th Cong., 3d Sess., Vol. VIII, No. 58. Washington.

Boilvin, Nickolas. Prairie du Chien in 1811. In Wis. Hist. Colls., XI.

Boyd, Indian Agent. Papers, 1832. In Wis. Hist. Colls., XII.

Brymner, Douglas. Capture of Fort McKay, Prairie du Chien, in 1814. In Wis. Hist. Colls., XI.

Calhoun, John C. Works. 6 vols. Edited by Richard K. Cralle. New York, 1888.

Canadian Archives, Papers from the, 1767–1814. In Wis. Hist. Colls., XII.

Canadian Archives, Papers from the, 1778–1783. In Wis. Hist. Colls., XI.

Carlier, Auguste. Condition Sociale des Indians : La République Américaine Etats-Unis. 4 vols. Paris, 1890.

Colby, L. W. The Sioux Indian War, 1890–91. In Reports of the Nebraska State Historical Society, III.

Commission, Report and Journal of the Proceedings of the, 1876. Senate Executive Documents, 44th Cong., 2nd Sess., Vol. 1, No. 9.

Commission, Report and Proceedings of the Sioux, 1887. Senate Documents, 51st Cong., 1st Sess., No. 51. Washington.

Commissioners of Indian Affairs, Report of, 1835–1894. 57 vols. Washington.

Congressional Globe, Containing the Debates and Proceedings of Congress, 1833–1873. 109 vols. Washington.

Council held by General Harney at Fort Pierre with Sioux Indians. Minutes. House Executive Documents, 34th Cong., 1st Sess., Vol. XII, No. 130. Washington.

Cruikshank, E. A. Robert Dickson, the Indian Trader. In Wis. Hist. Colls., XII.

Debates of Congress, Abridgment of the, 1789–1856. 15 vols. New York, 1857.

Dickson and Grignon Papers, 1812–1815.   In Wis. Hist. Colls., XI.

Dodge, R. I.   The Plains of the Great West.   New York, 1877.

Donaldson, Thomas.   The Public Domain : Its History, with Statistics. Washington, 1884.

Donaldson, Thomas.   The George Catlin Indian Gallery.   In Smithsonian Report, 1885, Part II.

Egleston, Melville.   The Land System of the New England Colonies. In J. H. U. Studies, IV.   Baltimore.

Estimates for Sioux Indians.   R. McClelland.   February 3, 1857.   House Miscellaneous Documents, 34th Cong., 3d Sess., Vol. I, No. 146. Washington.

Ethnology, Annual Reports of the Bureau of, 1879–1893.   14 vols. Washington.

Expenditures for Sioux Indians.   March 9, 1876.   House Miscellaneous Documents, 44th Cong., 1st Sess., Vol. V, No. 126.   Washington.

Flandrau, Chas. E.   The Inkpaduta Massacre of 1857.   In Minn. Hist. Colls., III.

Forsyth, Thomas.   Letter-Book.   In Wis. Hist. Colls., XI.

Fort Laramie.   Treaty of 1851.   Copy obtained from the Secretary of the Interior.   Washington, 1895.

Fort Snelling, Early Days at.   In Minn. Hist. Colls., I.

Fur Trade and Factory System at Green Bay, 1816–1821.   Largely made up of letters of Mathew Irwin, United States Factor, and Thomas L. McKenny, Superintendent of the Indian trade.   In Wis. Hist. Colls., VII.

Grattan Massacre.   Report on the Department of the West :   House Executive Documents, 33d Cong., 2d Sess., Vol. I, No. 1.   Washington.

Hampton Institute, 1868–1885.   Its Work for Two Races.   Hampton, 1885.

Hampton Institute, Ten Years' Work for Indians at.   Hampton, 1888.

Harney, W. S.   Report exhibiting the operations and results of the Sioux expedition under his command, September 5, 1855.   Senate Executive Documents, 34th Cong., 1st Sess., Vol. II, No. 1.   Washington.

Harrison, J. B.   The Latest Studies on Indian Reservations.   Philadelphia, 1887.

Heard, I. V. D.   History of the Sioux War and Massacres of 1862–1863. New York, 1865.

Hildreth, Richard.   The History of the United States of America. 6 vols.   New York, 1882.

Holst, H. von. The Constitutional and Political History of the United States. 8 vols. Chicago, 1877-1892.

Holst, H. von. John C. Calhoun. Boston, 1892.

Indians, Reports on, 1790-1834. Embodied in the Reports of the Secretary of War.

Indian Affairs, American State Papers, 1789-1827. 2 vols. Washington.

Indian Affairs, 1761-1800. In Mich. Pioneer and Hist. Colls., XX.

Indian Commissioners, Annual Reports of the Board of, 1869-1893. 25 vols. Washington.

Indian Rights Association, Annual Reports of the Executive Committee of, 1883-1893. 10 vols. Philadelphia.

Jackson, H. H. A Century of Dishonor. New York, 1881.

James, James Alton. English Institutions and the American Indian. Baltimore, 1894.

Jefferson, Thomas. Writings. 9 vols. Edited by H. A. Washington. Washington, 1853-4.

Kelley, W. F. The Indian Troubles and the Battle of Wounded Knee. In Reports of the Nebraska State Historical Society, IV.

Lands for Sioux Indians, Message on. President A. Johnson. June 9, 1866. House Executive Documents, 39th Cong., 1st Sess., Vol. XII, No. 126. Washington.

Lewis and Clark Expedition, History of. Faithfully reprinted from * * * Original Manuscript Journals and Field Notebooks of the Explorers. Edited by Elliott Coues. 4 vols. New York, 1893.

Lockwood, James H. Early Times and Events in Wisconsin. In Wis. Hist. Colls., II.

Lodge, Henry Cabot. George Washington. 2 vols. Boston and New York, 1890.

Manypenny, George W. Our Indian Wards. Cincinnati, 1880.

McMaster, John Bach. A History of the People of United States. 4 vols. New York, 1884-1895.

Meserve, Charles F. A Tour of Observation among Indians and Indian Schools. Philadelphia, 1894.

Message and Documents, Abridgment of. Entire set. Washington.

Michigan Pioneer and Historical Collections, 1874-1893. 22 vols. Published by the Michigan Pioneer and Historical Society. Lansing.

Minnesota Historical Society Collections. 8 vols. St. Paul, 1872-1893.

Mohonk, Proceedings of the Annual Conference, 1883-1893. 10 vols. Philadelphia.

Morgan, T. J. Indian Education.

Morgan, T. J. The Present Phase of the Indian Question. Boston, 1891.

Nebraska State Historical Society. Transactions and Reports, 1885-1893. 5 vols. Lincoln and Fremont.

Neill, E. D. Dakota Land and Dakota Life. In Minn. Hist. Colls., I.

Neill, E. D. History of the Ojibways and their Connection with Fur Traders, based upon Official and Other Records. In Minn. Hist. Colls., V.

Neill, E. D. Occurrences in and Around Fort Snelling, from 1819-1840. In Minn. Hist. Colls., III.

Niles' Weekly Register, containing Political, Historical, and Geographical * * * Documents, Essays and Facts, 1811-1849. 76 vols. From September, 1837, called Niles' National Register. Baltimore, 1811-1849.

Palmer, H. E. History of the Powder River Expedition of 1865. In Reports of the Nebraska State Historical Society, II.

Pancoast, Henry S. Impressions of the Sioux Tribes in 1882. Philadelphia, 1883.

Pancoast, Henry S. The Indian Before the Law. Philadelphia, 1884.

Parton, James. Life of Andrew Jackson. 3 vols. Boston and New York.

Peters, Richard. Report of Cases Argued and Adjudged in the Supreme Court of the United States, 1828-1842. 16 vols. Philadelphia.

Pike, Zebulon M. An Account of Expeditions to the Sources of the Mississippi and through the Western Parts of Louisiana. Philadelphia, 1810.

Powell, J. W. Indian Linguistic Families North of Mexico. In Report of the Bureau of Ethnology, 1885-86. Washington.

Prairie du Chien, Documents, 1814-1815. In Wis. Hist. Colls., IX.

Removal of the Indians. Documents and Proceedings relating to the * * * Emigration, Preservation, and Improvement of the Aborigines of America. In North American Review, XXX, 62-121.

Report on the Department of the West, September 7, 1854. House Ex. Docs., 33d Cong., 2d Sess., Vol. 1, No. 9.

Revised Statutes of United States. 3 vols. Washington, 1878-1891.

Roosevelt, Theodore. The Winning of the West. 2 vols. New York, 1889.

Roosevelt, Theodore. Thomas H. Benton. Boston and New York, 1890.

Roosevelt, Theodore. Report made to the United States Civil Service Commission upon a visit to certain Indian Reservations and Schools in South Dakota, Nebraska, and Kansas. Philadelphia, 1893.

Royce, Charles E. The Cherokee Nation of Indians. Report of the Bureau of Ethnology, 1883-84.

Schoolcraft, H. R. History, Condition, and Prospects of the Indian Tribes of the United States. 6 vols. Philadelphia, 1853-57.

Schoolcraft, H. R. History and Physical Geography of Minnesota. In Minn. Hist. Colls., I.

Schouler, James. History of the United States of America. 5 vols. New York.

Secretary of War, Reports of.

Sibley, H. H. Reminiscences: Historical and Personal. In Minn. Hist. Colls., I.

Sibley, H. H. Reminiscences of the Early Days of Minnesota. In Minn. Hist. Colls., III.

Sioux Expedition, Report on. W. S. Harney, September 5, 1855. Senate Executive Documents, 34th Cong., 1st Sess., Vol. II, No. 1.

Sioux Indians, Estimates for. R. McClelland. February 3, 1857. House Miscellaneous Documents, 34th Cong., 3d Sess., Vol. I, No. 46.

Sioux Indians, Minutes of a Council held by Gen. Harney with. House Executive Documents, 34th Cong., 1st Sess., Vol. XII, No. 130.

Sioux, Military Expedition Against, 1876. Executive Documents, 44th Cong., 1st Sess., Vol. XIV, No. 184.

Shaw, Albert. Our Indian Problem and How We Are Solving It. In Review of Reviews, June, 1892.

Statesman's Manual. Compiled by Edwin Williams. 2 vols. New York, 1846.

Street, Joseph M. Prairie du Chien in 1827. In Wis. Hist. Colls., XI.

Thayer, James B. The Dawes Bill and the Indians. In Atlantic Monthly, March, 1888.

Thayer, James B. A People Without a Law. In Atlantic Monthly, October, 1891.

Thwaites, Reuben G. American Fur Company Invoices, 1821-22. In Wis. Hist. Colls., XI.

Toqueville, Alexis De. Democracy in America. Translated by Reeve. 2 vols. Boston, 1873.

Treaties and Conventions between the United States and Other Powers, 1776-1887. Washington, 1889.

Turner, F. J. The Character and Influence of Indian Trade in Wisconsin. Baltimore, 1891.

United States Statutes at Large, 1789-1893. 27 vols. Boston and Washington, 1850-1893.

Walker, F. A. The Indian Question. Boston, 1874.

War of 1812. Copies of Papers on File in the Dominion Archives at

Ottawa, Canada, Pertaining to the Relations of the British Government with the United States.   In Mich. Pioneer Colls., XV, XVI.

Washington, George.   Writings.   Edited by Worthington Chauncey Ford.   14 vols.   New York and London, 1889.

Welsh, Herbert.   Civilization Among the Sioux Indians.   Philadelphia, 1893.

Welsh, Herbert.   How to Bring the Indian to Citizenship, and Citizenship to the Indian.   In Boston Commonwealth, April 9, 1892.

Welsh, Herbert.   The Indian Question, Past and Present.   In N. E. Mag., October, 1890.

Welsh, Herbert.   The Meaning of the Dakota Outbreak.   In Scribner's Magazine, April, 1891.

Wharton, Francis.   A Digest of the International Law of the United States.   3 vols.   Washington, 1886.

Wheaton, Henry.   Reports of Cases Argued and Adjudged in the Supreme Court of the United States, 1816–1827.   12 vols.   New York.

Williamson, T. S.   The Sioux or Dakotas.   In Minn. Hist. Colls., III.

Wisconsin Historical Collections.   12 vols.   Madison, 1855–1892.